IRA ALDRIDGE

Taras Shevchenko's Portrait of Ira Aldridge, 1858.

IRA ALDRIDGE

SERGEI N. DURYLIN

============== ⁓ ==============

Translated by Alexei Lalo
With an essay by Viktoria N. Toropova on Sergei N. Durylin
Edited by Bernth Lindfors

AFRICA WORLD PRESS
<small>TRENTON | LONDON | CAPE TOWN | NAIROBI | ADDIS ABABA | ASMARA | IBADAN</small>

AFRICA WORLD PRESS
541 West Ingham Avenue | Suite B
Trenton, New Jersey 08638

Copyright © 2014
Sergei N. Durylin, Ira Aldridge © Durylin Memorial House
Museum, Moscow
English translation © Alexei Lalo
Essay on "Sergei Nikolaevich Durylin" © Viktoria N. Toropova
Preface and editorial work © Bernth Lindfors

Cover design: Dapo Ojo-Ade

Library of Congress Cataloging-in-Publication Data

Durylin, S. N. (Sergei Nikolaevich), 1877-1954.
   Ira Aldridge / Sergei N. Durylin ; translated by Alexei Lalo ; with an essay by Viktoria N. Toropova on Sergei N. Durylin ; edited by Bernth Lindfors.
      pages cm
   Includes bibliographical references and index.
   ISBN 978-1-59221-980-3 (hard cover : alk. paper) -- ISBN 978-1-59221-981-0 (pbk. : alk. paper) 1. Aldridge, Ira Frederick, -1867.
2. Actors--United States--Biography. 3. African American actors--Biography. 4. African Americans--Europe--Biography.
5. Shakespearean actors and actresses--Biography. 6. Black theater--History. 7. Theater--Great Britain--History--19th century. I. Lalo, Alexei, translator. II. Lindfors, Bernth, editor. III. Title.
   PN2287.A457D8713 2014
   792.02'8092--dc23
   [B]
                                        2014014756

CONTENTS

===============☙===============

ILLUSTRATIONS

ACKNOWLEDGEMENTS

═ ═ ═ ═ ═ ═ ═ ═ ═ ═ ═ ═ ═ ═ CB ═ ═ ═ ═ ═ ═ ═ ═ ═ ═ ═ ═ ═ ═

First I wish to thank Gennadii Vasilievich Lebedev, Director of the Durylin Memorial House Museum, for encouraging this English translation of Durylin's biography of Ira Aldridge. The Museum, which holds the copyright on Durylin's archive and legacy, also supplied three photos and one portrait included in this volume.

Most of the rest of the illustrations, originally published as part of Durylin's book, came from the files of the Federal State Budget Institution of Culture "A.A. Bakhrushin Theater Museum" in Moscow, which holds the copyright on them. The replica of Shevchenko's portrait of Aldridge was provided by the Taras Shevchenko Museum in Toronto. The generous support of these two institutions is also gratefully acknowledged.

Next I must thank Victoria N. Toropova for having supplied an excellent summary of the life of career of Sergei Nikolaevich Durylin, a most remarkable scholar whose groundbreaking study of Aldridge remains the primary source of reliable information on the actor's activities in Russia.

Last but far from least, I am greatly in debt to Alexei Lalo for having translated the whole book in his spare time. He had worked for me earlier for several years as a translator of numerous documents relating to Aldridge's performances in Russia and Ukraine. Others who have assisted me in tasks of this kind include Lisa Strid, Marina Alexandrova, Anna Katsnelson, Katya Corey, Elena Zakrutaeva, Elena Liskova, Helen S. Pogosyan-Grigoriev, Marina Flider, Vladiyslav C. Alexander, and of course the late Herbert Marshall, who in a biography he co-authored with Mildred Stock entitled *Ira Aldridge: The Negro Tragedian* (1958), was the first to translate a portion of Durylin's pioneering scholarship on Aldridge into English. I mention this large team of translators because it is possible that some of their words have occasionally supplemented the fine work done by Alexei Lalo.

PREFACE

═══════════════ ⟡ ═══════════════

Sergei N. Durylin was the first scholar to attempt to write a biography of Ira Aldridge, the famous nineteenth-century actor, eventually publishing it in Russian in 1940. Viktoria N. Toropova tells us that it took him five years to do so, partly because he was engaged in many other interesting projects simultaneously. Durylin was a prolific savant throughout his career, but he turned to theater studies as the primary focus of his research in the last twenty years of his life. The book on Aldridge was just one of numerous seminal contributions he made as an emerging authority of Russia's rich theater history. Today, at Toropova attests, he is remembered as a pioneer who helped to establish theater studies as a scholarly discipline in Russia.

Writing on Aldridge would have been a challenging undertaking in the 1930s because the remarkable black tragedian, who died in 1867, had been forgotten in the interim. The few reference books that mentioned him were full of errors, and it was hard to find reliable information on his early life in America and his start as a professional actor in Britain. Aldridge began touring other parts of Europe in

1852, but it was not until he reached St. Petersburg in 1858, Moscow in 1862, and a large number of provincial cities and town in the few years that followed that Durylin could find the resources he needed to construct a trustworthy record of his accomplishments on the Russian stage.

As a consequence, his opening chapters focusing on Aldridge's life in North America, England, and Germany are weak, for they rely principally on a German translation of a biographical pamphlet published in London that mixed fiction with fact and sometimes got the facts wrong. But when Durylin turned his attention to Aldridge's activities in Russia, he suddenly was on solid ground for he had access to many old newspapers and actors' memoirs that contained authentic eyewitness reports telling what Aldridge did as a performer and how he was received by audiences. Durylin often provided useful background information on Aldridge's appearances in specific locations, but he allowed the responses of those who had actually seen him perform to tell the story of how he interpreted his roles and what they thought of his acting. Some of his chapters offer long strings of quotations taken from such documents. This was an effective way to present evidence of what Aldridge managed to achieve in his final years as a touring star. These voices from the past help us to understand the impact he made on his Russian contemporaries.

Durylin's scholarship on Aldridge remains influential not only in Russia but also in biographical research undertaken elsewhere. Herbert Marshall relied heavily on Durylin's findings when writing the Russian chapters of *Ira Aldridge: The Negro Tragedian* (1958), a biography he co-authored with Mildred Stock. Now that Durylin's entire book is finally available in English, I hope the Russian chapters will continue to serve as a model of how responsible biographical inquiries should be conducted.

Bernth Lindfors

INTRODUCTION

═ ═ ═ ═ ═ ═ ═ ═ ═ ═ ═ ═ ═ ═ ℭℬ ═ ═ ═ ═ ═ ═ ═ ═ ═ ═ ═ ═ ═ ═

*I*ra Aldridge is among those actors forgotten in the history of theater. Although here in Russia several touching reminiscences about him have been preserved in various memoirs and no significant encyclopedia has omitted his name, in the country of Shakespeare, of whose dramas Aldridge was one of the best interpreters, he has not even been noticed by having an entry in *The Encyclopedia Britannica*.[1] Nor is his name mentioned in another world-famous encyclopedia—the French *La Grande Encyclopedie*.[2] Instead of providing a biography of the renowned actor, most recent American and British encyclopedias cite some unreliable data about his life.[3] In the *National American*

---

1 Aldridge is not mentioned in the ninth edition of *The Encyclopedia Britannica* (Edinburgh, 1875-89) nor in the Index. He is not in *The New Volumes of the Encyclopedia Britannica* (Edinburgh and London, 1902) either.

2 *La Grande Encyclopedie* (Paris, 1886-1902). Aldridge is also absent from the Italian *Enciclopedia Italiana di scienze, lettere ed arti* (Milan, 1929-36).

3 Two prominent contemporary encyclopedias, the American *The New International Encyclopedia* and the British *Chamber's*

Biographical Encyclopedia (New York, 1906) his name is absent altogether; he evidently was deemed unworthy of being included in the pantheon of British celebrities. The so-called *Der Grosse Brockhaus* devotes two lines to Aldridge, and even those contain mistakes.[4] One may get the impression that European and American theater scholars have all joined in a conspiracy of silence against the famous black tragedian. It is significant that when the American journal *The Crisis*, an official publication of the National Association for the Advancement of Colored People, released an issue on the protection of cultural rights of Negroes and wanted to include an article on Aldridge, it contacted a Soviet theater scholar. The American ones were of no help.[5]

It is no surprise then that an early biography of Aldridge, covering his American and British years, does not exist. His father's occupation is defined differently by various commentators. Some say he was a ship carpenter; others call him a pastor of princely descent. The great tragedian's date of birth varies in these sources between 1807 and 1827.[6] His place of birth is found in two parts of the world—North America and Africa, and those who select America arbitrarily choose between New York, Bel Air, and

---

Encyclopedia, both published in 1930, cite different "beginnings" for Aldridge. The former (2 ed. New York, 1: 368) tells us that Aldridge was born in North America, in Bel Air, in 1810, while the latter (New ed., London and Edinburgh, 1:142) claims he was born in 1803 in Senegambia, Africa.

4 *Der Grosse Brockhaus* (Leipzig, 1929), 258. In the 1926 edition of *Handbuch des Wissens: Brockhaus,* Aldridge is not mentioned.

5 Sergius Kara-Mourza. "Ira Aldridge in Russia" *The Crisis* 40 (September 1933): 201-2. American and British sources of Aldridge's biography are striking in their scantiness.

6 *Deutsches Theaterlexicon,* ed. Adolf Oppenheim und Ernst Gettke (Leipzig, 1889), 24.

Baltimore. In the absence of a credible biographical foundation for studying his activities in America and Britain, one has to randomly choose the most probable events and discard those that are obviously absurd. The Russian period of Aldridge's life is the one best documented. Aldridge's biography can now be narrated only with many reservations and the inevitable anticipation of future correctives that will eliminate a lot of misinformation about his life.

IN NORTH AMERICA

═ ═ ═ ═ ═ ═ ═ ═ ═ ═ ═ ═ ═ ═ ◌ℨ ═ ═ ═ ═ ═ ═ ═ ═ ═ ═ ═ ═ ═ ═

*T*he opening chapter of Aldridge's biography unwittingly leads one to think of a strange parallel between the actor's life and that of his favorite character. As Othello first enters the stage and addresses Iago, he says,

> I fetch my life and being
> From men of royal siege... (Act 1, Scene 2)

In 1858 Ye. F. Yunge, introducing Taras G. Shevchenko to Aldridge's life story, rendered it in the following way, citing Aldridge's own testimony: "His father was a son of some African petty tsar."[1] According to Aldridge's own account, his ancestors were chiefs of the Fulah tribe that lived on the shores of Senegal, on Africa's western coast. Influenced by an American missionary, his grandfather suggested to his belligerent fellow tribesmen that they should not sell their

---

1 Ye.F. Yunge, *Vospominaniya 1843-1860* (Memoirs of Ye.F. Yunge, née Countess Tolstaya, 1843-1863) (St. Petersburg: Sphinx, 1913), 168. Yunge's memoir (she was for several years a close friend and confidante of Aldridge) is one of the most valuable sources for his biography.

prisoners of war into slavery but rather hold them to ransom. This suggestion was contrary to the customs of the tribe and caused indignation among the tribesmen. Aldridge's grandfather was killed along with nearly all his family. The only one who escaped was Daniel, his son; he was rescued by the missionary and brought to America. The missionary was from the North where there was no blatant slavery, and his foster son was therefore considered "free." The young Negro was converted to Christianity and studied at a divinity college near New York before he was sent to Africa as a missionary.

In Baltimore, probably around 1805 (no exact date is known), Daniel Aldridge's son was born; his name was Ira Frederick. There is a theory that missionary work had never cured Daniel Aldridge of the notion of becoming an African prince. When the "usurper of the throne" died, he tried to re-establish himself among his people as their king and convert his subjects to the Christian faith. He succeeded in neither. In Africa certain events took place, about which Aldridge could have narrated in Othello's words:

> Of moving accidents by flood and field,
> Of hair-breadth 'scapes i' the imminent deadly breach,
> Of being taken by the insolent foe
> And sold to slavery; of my redemption thence
> And portance in my traveler's history;
> Wherein of antres vast and deserts idle…(Act 1, Scene 3).

Aldridge could give an account of all this, as his father with all his family had to wander about the hostile country. Ira Aldridge recalled that "once, as an eight-year-old, he was playing near the door of their shack, and saw several soldiers passing by. They saw his resemblance to the fugitive chief, Ira's father, whose whereabouts had been unknown to them. The shack's owner was interrogated and told them that this was her daughter's son, [so] the soldiers left them alone."[2] After long wanderings, the family returned to America. His childhood continued there. He grew up among black slaves, suffering the same way they did. Aldridge cherished hopes for his people's bright, free future. He was one of those who affirmed his people's right for a better role in the history of humankind. Throughout his life, Aldridge maintained a connection with his persecuted kinsmen and actively contributed to the black slaves' fight for their liberation. One of Aldridge's Russian biographers, who met with him in 1864, wrote: "Ever since the renewal of the black people's struggle for freedom, the famous tragedian has given away half of his income—that is, of all his performance honoraria—to a fund established for the cause of liberating the slaves. This constant contribution characterizes the moral and civil development of an artist and a human being."[3] One cannot understand Aldridge's art and evaluate his life's work without recognizing this lively

---

2 Anon. *Leben und Künstler-Laufbahn des Negers Ira Aldridge* (Berlin: Allgemeine Deutsche Verlags-Unstalt, 1853), 7-10. This booklet is based on Aldridge's own account when he was on tour in Berlin in 1853. Many excerpts are actually parenthesized in the book, which means that the author was quoting Aldridge's exact words. [Actually, the booklet was a translation of the anonymous *Memoir and Theatrical Career of Ira Aldridge, the African Roscius* (London: Onwhyn, [1848]), composed with the collaboration of Aldridge during his tours of the British Isles in the late 1840s. Other Aldridge quotes cited by Durylin also come from this source. Ed.]

3 N. Almedingen, "Po povodu ozhidaemogo priezda v Saratov Oldridzha (Regarding Aldridge's Upcoming Arrival in Saratov)," *Spravochny Listok* (Saratov Newsletter) 141 (1854).

connection, his blood brotherhood with the fate of "black people."

Aldridge was born in a state that was on the border of the slaveholding South and the free North. Up until 1789 North America was a colony of England and supplied it with cheap raw materials (cotton, cane sugar, wheat, leather), receiving in return finished products from England's highly developed industry. The War of Independence (1775-89) led to a form of political independence that was needed mostly by Northern states that had long before embarked on a path of developing their own industrial economy. This development was hampered by England's economic power that relied upon North America as merely a supplier of raw materials and consumer of English merchandise. Southern states, on the contrary, being largely agricultural, continued to value their connection with England, which was a market that consumed their raw materials.

During the Revolutionary War, out of two million Americans, about five hundred thousand were black slaves. Industrial development in the Northern states required free qualified labor, which was why they moved to abolish slavery, although the condition of Negroes remained very difficult there as well. In 1800, not long before Aldridge was born, there were around five million people living in America, of which 2.6 million lived in the North, and only 100,000 of them were Negroes. Meanwhile, of the 2.4 million living in the South, half were black slaves. In order to produce large quantities of cheap cotton, sugar, and wheat to export to England and other countries, the South needed cheap slave labor and therefore remained a fierce slaveholding region. Industrial England was interested in cheap American raw materials and knew very well that the main reason they were so cheap was the labor of black slaves. Thus, when in 1861 the war between the North and South began, enlightened English lords and factory owners sided with the slaveholding southern states and supported them in every way possible, employing all methods, right up to supplying military contraband.

England's friendship with the slaveholding states left an imprint on Aldridge's biography. The slave-owners created a "doctrine" about the black race's "unfitness" for European civilization and culture. The false assertion that a Negro, as a representative of a "lower" race, was not much different from an animal and was fit only for crude physical labor, was utilized by slaveholders to claim and justify their right to dominate black people. Any Negro who demonstrated intelligence and talent in the arts, sciences, or technology—a Negro artist, writer or doctor—served as a live refutation of this race theory. Hence, slaveholders and their allies felt hatred toward those like Aldridge who clearly refuted their theories, and this led to the persecutions he and others suffered in America and in England.

Daniel Aldridge, Ira's father, was a pastor in a special church for the "black-skinned." He was readying his son to become his successor because priesthood was the only occupation that gave a Negro a slim hope for personal safety. Aldridge's family had experienced the horrors of the existence of the so-called "free" Negro; the tragedian's brother was subjected to "lynching" in New Orleans in 1848, due to a petty spat with a white person at a card table. "No investigation was conducted," Aldridge would later bitterly complain, "No legal proceedings were initiated: after all, it was just a Negro!"

While still in grade school, Aldridge always received awards for declamation and passionately dreamed of seeing a theatrical performance. But this was not at all easy for a Negro. "At that time," as Aldridge would later recall, "there was a sign at a theater entrance: 'Dogs and negroes not allowed.'" To what extent this humiliating rule was observed can be seen even now, one hundred years later, in Washington, the U.S. capital city: "Negroes are not allowed into the cinemas (except for several small movie theaters for the 'colored') nor to theaters, even when Negro theater performances are on."[4]

In Aldridge's time there was only one group of seats in the upper circle of a theater, into which Negroes could sneak. There, next to tramps and pickpockets, Ira first saw a theater performance on stage. It produced a huge impression on him. Ira vowed to himself that he would become an actor playing in the language of the whites—that is, in English—in works by white authors. It was a plucky dream. A Negro could not watch white actors play, whereas Aldridge dreamed of acting for white spectators.

Despite various misfortunes and numerous obstacles, despite his (albeit slight) stuttering, Ira Aldridge craved the glory of an actor. Obsessed with his dream of the stage, he moved straight toward his established goal. For his debut, he studied the part of Rolla in the then popular tragedy by Richard Brinsley Sheridan (1751-1816), *Pizarro* (1799), which was set in South America, in Peru.[5] Clearly, Aldridge's debut could only take place on a private stage, with a small

---

4 Anon. "[Correspondence from Washington]," *Izvestia VTSIK* 152 (June 30, 1935).

5 This tragedy was well known in Russia. Pimen Nikolaevich Arapov, in his *Letopis Russkago Teatra* (Chronicle of the Russian Theater) (St. Petersburg: Tip N. Tiblena i komp, 1861), points to a performance of the historical drama *Pizarro , or the Conqueror of Peru* in St. Petersburg on August 17, 1819.

amateur troupe, where there was not a single white actor. As Aldridge himself would later recount, the tragedy's heroine, "the beautiful Cora, was so black that quite a bit of makeup—white, yellow and red—was necessary to give her cheeks the hues of roses and lilies with which Sheridan had endowed her."

The performance of *Pizarro*, and especially that of Aldridge as Rolla, had such great success that, inspired by it, Aldridge decided to realize his most cherished dream—to play in a Shakespearean tragedy. The young Negro actor played the role of Romeo and then dared to do Hamlet. His performances enjoyed growing success. Acting in Shakespearean plays, Aldridge refused to wear white makeup—both he himself and his whole troupe. A black Romeo could have his own black Juliet, he was thinking. So to the Yankees' greatest indignation, he played the black-skinned Romeo. This was not a whim of a talented youngster but his recognition of his race's right to participate in world art.

Young Aldridge's performances of the most difficult Shakespearean roles were far from perfect, but his talent and passionate love of Shakespeare helped him to convey much of the sublime. Aldridge's success in these roles caused professional envy among white actors and the hatred of those who saw Negroes as something midway between human beings and animals. Slander poured upon the black Hamlet and Romeo. They tried to ridicule not just the black actor but also black spectators, arguing that neither could get even close to understanding Shakespeare.

In 1822, when young Aldridge first acted in Shakespeare's roles, a famous English actor, Charles Mathews (1776-1835), was touring North America. He became interested in the Negro actor and attended one of his performances. Aldridge would later describe this visit:

> Mathews came to see an evening performance, and this later served him well to create one of his most amusing anecdotes in his sketch "A Trip to America." He claims that when I, as Hamlet, was delivering the famous monologue "To be or not to be" and reached the point when I said, "And, by opposing, end them," the audience thought that I said a similar-sounding line from a Negro song, "Possum Up a Gum Tree," and they noisily demanded that I perform this song. Ostensibly, Mathews responded to this request by having me say, "Well, ladies and gentlemen, obviously you like the song 'Possum Up a Gum Tree' more than *Hamlet*. I will sing it, fine." And, according to Mathews's account, I did sing this song three or four times, to the great exhilaration and enjoyment of the black audience, and then I allegedly continued my performance as Hamlet! Perhaps I should not even bother to add that the anecdote narrated by Mr. Mathews had nothing to do with reality.

Such anecdotes were contrived by the whites to show that the black actor and black spectators were too ignorant to appreciate Shakespeare.

A German biographer quotes Aldridge's words:

> Real Yankees could not imagine how one could allow such things as Negroes—or "niggers"—acting in white Shakespearean roles, as their cursed impudence and monstrous impertinence were completely unnatural. Stephen Price, a well-known theater entrepreneur, was envious of the success of the "real Ethiopian" and sent his agents to obstruct his work. The Negroes had begun attracting a lot of attention, and many of those who had initially scorned them, turned into their admirers. Instigated by Price's agents, street disturbances began, and the small theater was wrecked and looted. It was

impossible to obtain protection or compensation from the police (for they of course were white), and the troupe was scattered.[6]

But Aldridge's passion for the theater was so great that he could not endure abandoning it. Helped by a former schoolmate who carried costumes to Chatham Theatre for an actor named Wallack, Aldridge gained access to this theater, and when his comrade died, he managed to take this job of his. His only purpose was to retain the right to sneak in behind the scenes and breathe the atmosphere of the theater. Ira received no remuneration for doing this work for Wallack and other actors. He was happy only to be able to see the actors play each evening and learn from their craft. As a famous actor much later, Aldridge loved to recall that he would lean against a wing and inhale the intoxicating joy of the theater, ecstatically listening to the stream of words spoken on the stage. He would then become filled with hope that one day he would also be able to compete with the greatest actors.

Aldridge's father decided to put an end to this theatrical enthusiasm of his son, who could not bear to miss an opportunity to serve even as a lackey in order to get access to a white theater. Under the patronage of two bishops, Ira was admitted to the same divinity college near New York from which his father had graduated. Ira was an excellent student there, but he would never forget his true vocation, not for one minute. An actor, not a pastor—that was the choice he had made once and forever.

The prospect of seeing his son become an actor frightened Aldridge's father for he could not forget the furious mob destroying the small theater where black actors,

---

6 *Leben und Künstler-Laufbahn des Negers Ira Aldridge*, 13-16.

headed by his son, had performed. In order to shield Ira from the sad destiny of a black actor in slaveholding America, Daniel Aldridge decided upon a drastic measure. He sent his son to do his studies in Europe, in Glasgow. There, he thought, in a new country, in different life conditions, Ira's dream of the stage would fade away, and he would replace it by becoming a theology scholar. The father of the great actor was horribly mistaken.

IN ENGLAND AND GERMANY

================ CB ================

At Glasgow University the same American college story repeated itself: Aldridge attended all the lectures diligently, studying Shakespeare and Schiller. He mastered Latin so well that he could write easily in it, but of all the subjects, he took most interest in declamation, dreamt of acting on stage, and secretly prepared for performing one role after another.

Finally, in 1826 Aldridge overcame great difficulties to get a debut at the Royalty Theatre, a small playhouse in East London. He decided to perform a part that would allow him to display his black face openly, a role in which white actors needed to blacken their faces. Ira debuted as Othello with great success. He wanted to believe that England did not have the same obstacles for a black actor that had blocked him from a stage career in America. He was next invited to the Coburg Theatre, where he had tremendous success. But, acting alongside white actors, he only could play Negroes, mulattoes, and Moors. Aldridge wished to play Shakespearean roles as well, but apart from Othello, he was allowed to perform only Aaron the Moor in *Titus Andronicus*. Aldridge realized that a black actor in England, as in America, must win the right to play whites—and he firmly made up his mind to do that. Meanwhile, his Othello began enjoying repeated success.

During this time he also happened to play a version of the first act of Othello in real life. "At one of Aldridge performances, when he was acting as Gambia in *The Slave*, he was invited to the box of an influential lord who represented Berkshire in Parliament. This lord's daughter, almost like a new Desdemona, decided to leave everything in her life behind to be with Aldridge. Six weeks later she was already his wife. At the meeting with her family he literally recited Othello's lines to them:

> That I have ta'en away this old man's daughter,
> It is most true. True, I have married her. (Act 1, Scene 3)"[1]

The lord then had to play the part of the Venetian senator Brabantio: he had to put up with this marriage. His daughter played the part of Desdemona to the very end, but without the tragic finale: she would faithfully accompany Aldridge in all his wanderings.

Unable to obtain a permanent, full-time engagement in London, Aldridge spent several years in the provinces, acting on different stages. Those were the final years of his "apprenticeship," the years of "travels." Yet despite the favorable impression produced by the "African Keene," as he came to be called in London, it took some time for Aldridge to get his first engagement in Dublin. Initially no letters could persuade Calcraft, director of the local theater, to dare hire the black-skinned actor; there was something absurd about it, in his opinion. Then Aldridge went to

---

1   K.I. Zvantsov, *Ira Aldridge: Essay on His Life and Performances* (St. Petersburg: Ya. Ionson, 1858), 9.

Dublin at his own expense, met Calcraft, and managed to achieve the goal of acting in several performances at that theater. At that time Dublin was expecting the arrival of the great tragedian Edmund Kean. Calcraft tried to persuade Aldridge not to play Othello, as Kean did not like it when someone would play his favorite parts not long before his own performances. Aldridge was offered a debut in the role of Zanga in *The Revenge* instead, but he did not agree and played Othello there in December, 1831. This was the first time he played in such a large theater.

In Ireland's capital, more so than in London, Aldridge had fantastic success. Everyone was especially captivated by his facial expressions in Othello. A critic for a local newspaper testified that "The actor's dark face [Aldridge played Othello without makeup. S.D.] was a mirror reflecting a roaring storm, his soul tortured by the lightning movements of passion." Aldridge could feel satisfied: a white critic had hailed him as a "genius of theater arts."[2] But in Dublin, despite his success, Aldridge was allowed to play only in a limited number of productions; a permanent position for a black tragedian in a troupe of white actors was considered inadmissible. Aldridge had to let Edmund Kean replace him, after which the "African Keene" left for a remote province.

In Aldridge's life and theatrical career the role of Edmund Kean (1787-1833), like that of his son and stage successor, Charles (1811-1868), is unclear. The range of biographical contradictions here is as wide as that in determining Aldridge's year of birth. According to one version, Edmund Kean was Aldridge's theatrical mentor; the young Negro actor was allegedly the English tragedian's personal secretary during his tour of America and left for

---

2 *Leben und Künstler-Laufbahn des Negers Ira Aldridge*, 22-23.

Europe with him in order to become an actor. This version, recounted in the most recent *Dictionary of American Biography*, is of dubious credibility.[3] Other versions, closer to reality, do not support this idyll of a creative personal relationship between the English and Negro tragedians. J. Fitzgerald Molloy, the author of *The Life and Adventures of Edmund Kean* (London: Ward and Downey, 1888), describes Kean's trip to America in detail but does not even mention him meeting Aldridge there. Also, in the most recent American biography of Kean, Harold N. Hillebrand's *Edmund Kean* (New York: Columbia University Press, 1933), two chapters (the 9th and 12th) are devoted to Kean's trips to North America, but neither chapter mentions Kean's meeting with Aldridge, the latter's serving as Kean's secretary, or anything at all about Kean's patronage of the black actor. Aldridge's very name is absent from this book.

German and Russian authors of biographical essays on Aldridge who socialized with him during his tours of Germany and Russia—the countries where he enjoyed most success and recognition as an actor and a human being—are silent about this relationship, while Aldridge himself, usually so willing to recount his life story to his Russian friends, said nothing whatsoever about Kean's patronage. On the contrary, here is what his longtime friend Ye. F. Yunge (in whose father's house Aldridge was always received as a member of the family) recalls from his stories: "how much suffering he had had to go through and how much energy he had needed to expend before he managed to become famous—and not even in his own motherland. Even in England prejudices against the black race were so strong that the actor Kean (son or grandson of the famous

---

3 *Dictionary of American Biography*, ed. Allen Johnson (London: Humphrey Milford, 1928), 1: 160-61.

actor, I don't remember for sure), having learned that Aldridge had an engagement with the same theater where he worked, indignantly refused to act on the same stage with the 'contemptible Negro.'"[4]

This was Charles Kean, Edmund's son, who was a well-known actor at that time. It is hard to imagine that the father's attitude to Aldridge was drastically different from that of his son. During his Dublin tour the elder Kean saw Aldridge as Othello and recommended him to an entrepreneur from a provincial town, writing to him that "the performances of the black Roscius were a great delight," and that he was "quite artful," but immediately qualifying this by adding the ambiguous reservation that Aldridge "will prove successful under your judicious guidance" and that Kean himself "would become Kean again in a day or two"—that is, he would ensure his acting would make everyone forget Aldridge.[5]

Edmund Kean had to cease being himself to recognize Aldridge's art. Their acting styles were opposite to one another—and so were their respective fates. Kean gained wealth and fame by touring everywhere; all the theaters worldwide opened their doors to him, whereas Aldridge had to face closed doors. Aldridge ran away from America, while Kean went there to rake in heaps of money. Their manner of acting also differed. Kean was close to the Russian actor Mochalov. He was an actor-romantic, with the same strengths and weaknesses, but without the brilliant democratic dimension of Mochalov's creative work.

---

4   Yunge, *Vospominaniya*, 168. Talking about his descent and his childhood with his friends the Tolstoys, Aldridge confirms the version I am using in my book.

5   *Leben und Künstler-Laufbahn des Negers Ira Aldridge*, 23. Zvantsov, *Ira Aldridge*, 10.

Tumultuous explosions in Kean's acting at certain moments were followed by a dull recitation of boring text, through which he dragged himself sluggishly without being interested in the play, up until a new explosion of passion would shake up the theater, only to be followed by another switch to dull monotony. A character played by Kean would thus break apart into several shining fragments, absolutely unconnected and not cemented together as a whole being.

George Henry Lewes, in writing about Kean, said,

> The irregular splendour of his power was felicitously characterised in the saying of Coleridge, that 'seeing Kean act was reading Shakspeare by flashes of lightning,' so brilliant and so startling were the sudden illuminations, and so murky the dull intervals. Critics who had formed their ideal on the Kemble school were shocked at Kean's want of dignity, and at his fitful elocution, sometimes thrillingly effective, at other times deplorably tame and careless; in their angry protests they went so far as to declare him 'a mere mountebank.' Not so thought the pit; not so thought less biased critics. He stirred the general heart with such a rush of mighty power, impressed himself so vividly by accent, look and gesture, that it was as vain to protest against his defects as it was for French critics to insist upon Shakspeare's want of *bienséance* and *bon goût*."[6]

Aldridge as an actor was his direct opposite. While he had a huge temperament, he was not an improviser of his role but its sculptor and architect. His characters were always built on a firm foundation of a deep psychological study of the given character and were notable for a complete artistic refinement of all details and parts of the character as

---

6 George Henry Lewes. *Actors and the Art of Acting.* Translated by F. Pavlov (Warsaw, 1876), 7-8.

a whole. This did not preclude but, rather, contributed to the emotional strength of his characters. Creating his parts, Aldridge consciously moved toward a poetic embodiment of the character on the basis of its realistic portrayal. Kean, quite the opposite, was an actor of idealistic romanticism who impressed with the force of tragic improvisation but at the same time was incapable of finding a solid realistic foundation for a part. The drastic contrast between Kean and Aldridge was especially conspicuous in the role of Othello. Othello as a calm loving husband, Othello as a military commander and state leader, was not successfully portrayed by Kean at all. Even those who found Aldridge's Othello overly realistic in the jealousy scenes would recognize that the first act, with its famous speech in the Senate, was full of sublime truth and calm beauty.

Aldridge's enemies accused him of naturalism, of distorting Shakespeare, of lowering and simplifying his characters. They could not forgive him for the deep truth that destroyed cold conventional grandeur or the tumultuous hyperbolism of previous stage interpretations of Shakespeare. Aldridge established a new approach to Shakespeare on the English stage, closer to realism than the old romanticism. Aldridge replaced excessiveness and grotesqueness of emotions, fanciful solemnity of movements, with an in-depth understanding of Shakespearean personages, a careful study of their complex personalities, and a wonderful expressiveness of gesture and movement. Aldridge's Shakespearean characters powerfully captured the spectators' emotion and no less powerfully gave food for their thought. For Aldridge, Shakespeare was not just a realistic portrayer of life but also a deep thinker who enriched his audience with a knowledge of human beings and their place in life and in history. Aldridge liberated Shakespeare from the rich mantle in which he had still been robed since the seventeenth century, but he also tore off the romantic cloak with which some had tried to replace the worn-out mantle.

This irrationality of English actors' animosity toward Aldridge was based on another, more important, social factor. To accept a new, deeper treatment of Shakespeare in his own country from a Negro implied recognizing that this Negro had now a greater right to possess one of the treasures of European culture than English people themselves. In other words, this meant recognizing the absurdity of discussions about "lower" races.

In the years he spent in the provinces Aldridge developed a number of new roles in Shakespeare's *The Merchant of Venice* and *Richard III*, as well as in Schiller's *The Robbers* and *Fiesco's Conspiracy at Genoa*.

In 1833, after long and hard efforts, Aldridge finally appeared as Othello in London's large Covent Garden Theatre. The part of Desdemona was played by Ellen Tree (1805-1880), a well-known actress and the future wife of Charles Kean. Aldridge's success was great. At the end of the performance the audience stood up from their seats and threw their kerchiefs and hats in the air; rounds of applause did not stop for quite a while. Aldridge performed at Covent Garden four times and invariably scored a huge success with the public. Then suddenly his name disappeared from playbills. Even before the first performance, a disgusting campaign against the black tragedian had begun, and now it noticeably intensified after Aldridge's triumph on the stage of one of London's most renowned theaters.

White American actors who played at Covent Garden carried their contemptuous attitude toward Negroes to England from their slaveholding days in America. Small actors whose only "advantage" was the whiteness of their skin bullied the great actor as an inferior being who could not be tolerated in "decent" society. Most English actors shared this derogatory attitude to the Negro rival who eclipsed them with his talent in performing Shakespeare. Aldridge was at the receiving end of persecution inside and outside the theater. His partner, Ellen Tree, was accused of committing a crime against European culture, profaning art, and defiling the honor code of the performer.

Aldridge's defamation continued in the press. A number of London papers came close to accusing him of insulting Shakespeare, England's national hero. A black-skinned actor had no right to touch Shakespeare—that was the slogan British actors and journalists put forward against Aldridge. The persecution resulted in the doors of Covent Garden Theatre being shut in his face.

Aldridge did not give up. Using support from a certain portion of the public and the press, he moved to the smaller Surrey Theatre, but even there his performances lasted for only two evenings. Aldridge had to leave London and return to the provinces, where he resumed a nomadic life in very difficult conditions. His brilliant talent always attracted spectators, but the stigma of being a Negro deprived him of an opportunity to secure a full-time position at any prominent theater.

Aldridge made yet another attempt to reappear in London in 1848, at the very same Surrey Theatre. This time the public, influenced by a hostile press, shunned his performances. In a widely available humor magazine, *Punch*, an ironic note entitled "Ira est furor brevis" was published. The author played on the ambiguity of the word "Ira." Aldridge's first name in English meant "rage, ire" in Latin. In translation the statement became "Ire is short-time rage (or fury)." *Punch* said, "Theatre critics shower praises on one Mr. Aldridge, a real Ethiopian tragedian, who goes under the unusual name of *Ira*, which is undoubtedly very symbolic, for someone who bears it produces a *furor* everywhere he goes."[7] The statement seemed to be favorable toward Aldridge: Ira everywhere produces a furor. But one just has to read the word *Ira* in Latin in order to understand it as suggesting that "Ira Aldridge's fury throws the audience into the miserable condition of madness or rage (*furor*) but, fortunately, only for a short time (*brevis*)." The assumption is that the audience will soon get over this insane enthusiasm for the Negro actor.

Aldridge soon left London for the third time. The black tragedian carried his lot with great dignity, but his fate reflected the even more grievous lot of his race. Nonetheless, he received great support from an unexpected source. The lower chamber of the black republic of San Domingo on the island of Haiti in Central America honored Aldridge, stating that by his artistic activity he refuted the prejudice about a Negro's inability to understand European culture. The chamber endowed him with the title of Adjutant to the President of the Republic.

After continuing to perform in England, Scotland, and Ireland, Aldridge decided to try his luck abroad too. In the 1850s he toured with an English troupe in Central Europe, playing in Switzerland, France, Belgium, Austria, Hungary, and Sweden. His success was such that he often received official recognition in the form of various awards and medals. Aldridge was particularly well received and recognized by the public and critics in Germany. At that time there were numerous small kingdoms, duchies, and principalities in Germany. Their economic and political ties

---

7 *Leben und Künstler-Laufbahn des Negers Ira Aldridge*, 23-32.

with North America were insignificant, and, unlike England, they were not interested in perpetuating vestiges of slavery. In Germany Shakespeare was loved and well-known, so Aldridge's performances were received extremely well. Audiences there found novelty and value in his interpretations of tragic roles. He often was equated with the greatest actors in the world.

Aldridge was particularly triumphant in Berlin. After his first appearance as Othello there on January 3, 1853, a Berlin newspaper reported that

> Aldridge as Othello, with his natural black looks, is such a brilliant phenomenon that he should have a bright future, similar to the brilliant career of Rachel....The savage realism, glowing and sparkling in burning colors, with which Aldridge performed the Moor aroused to jealousy, deserves the highest praise. His gaze and gestures are clear interpreters of the artist speaking a foreign language; his face is the fiery mirror of his soul. The spectator forgets that he is in a theater, feels involuntarily seized, gripped, torn into the maelstrom of passions which wells up in the artist's eyes, roars in his natural tones, ripples in the nervous trembling of his hand. He was passionately called for an encore before and after Act 3, as well as at the end of the tragedy. And the tremendous applause was the expression of the public's *genuine* feeling of delight.

A critic at *Preussiche Zeitung* placed Aldridge as the best performer of Othello in Europe:

> After this Othello, what a punishment, what a hard test it is to have to see another one, a more conventional Othello! Passion, beauty, grandeur of aspiration—these are the three elements without which Othello is not a truly Shakespearean heroic character. Not a single actor was able to connect these three elements together and let us feel any of them in their entirety. We needed a Negro from

Africa's Western coast to appear and imprint the most magnificent and sublime artistic male image upon our imagination.

Analyzing Aldridge's performance in the scene with Iago (Act 3, Scene 3), the critic stated that "If Shakespeare himself were to play this scene as he intended it, he would have to play it just like Aldridge, even in its smallest details." The critic concluded by saying, "If Aldridge could play Hamlet as brilliantly, or any other Shakespearean character for whom his nature was not so well suited, then he would be not the 'African Roscius' but the greatest of all actors."

Aldridge did not hesitate to turn this expectation into reality. He immediately performed Macbeth, a role demanding totally different natural qualities and acting skills, a role in which his southern nature presumably could only prevent him from becoming a severe, reserved warrior from a foggy northern country. The way he played this Scottish king showed that he was as proficient in this role as he was in playing the "Venetian Moor." Critics wrote rapturous reviews of his Macbeth. The actor's main merit was said to be the fact that his Macbeth "shines with the deepest understanding of Shakespeare."

Aldridge stunned Berliners with his ability to conquer both the mountain heights of tragedy and master the sunny valleys of comedy. Regarding his appearance as the Negro Mungo in the light comedy *The Padlock*, the critics recalled Plato's statement in his *Symposium*: "A great tragedian must at the same time be a great comedian if the actor is to be like the poet." Aldridge played the simple-minded Negro servant in such a fashion that, according to one critic, "even the old chandeliers shake with laughter, and the gas flames shake with laughter." Reflecting general enthusiasm for

Aldridge's powerful gifts and highlighting his importance as a brilliant stage interpreter of Shakespeare, the Prussian Academy of Sciences and Arts awarded him an honorary membership.

Aldridge was really excited about the reception he had in Germany. In parting with the Berlin public, he bid farewell in a special epilogue that he himself had written, delivering it at the Royal Theater on January 13, 1853. After first addressing his audience in German, he recited his piece in verse, revealing to them circumstances of his own history:

> I am the son of a country whose tribe knows only the thirst for blood and mortal combat....Not yet awake from mental night, this lonely human tribe wanders around without knowing peace. I, born at a deserted seashore, managed to find the light of knowledge in a better country. Just as the sun rising over the waves breaks the shackles of night, a dark cloud has melted under these soft rays, and the spirit of a savage who is also human, a son of the human race, has flared up brightly, his soul humbled before the greatness of the world.

But the greatest thing in the world was theater, was tragedy. "My heart," Aldridge continued, "perceived the glittering characters of tragedy. Thrilled and enthused, my youthful imagination picked up one of these sacred flowers [recalling his first performance in *Romeo and Juliet*. S.D.], and a miracle ensued: in a passionate thirst for glory, I rushed to wanderings, although nature did not give any of the lilies and roses to my face that you possess. With a black face, a child of the sun, I stand here before you, but there is light in my soul."

It is difficult to determine whether Berlin critics truly were able to appreciate the striking sincerity and depth of these confessions, which spoke of his burning love for the great art of Shakespeare that belongs to all of humanity. Exiled from America, exhausted by persecution in England, Aldridge finished his speech with a touching word of gratitude: "I came to you as a lonely wanderer....Your warm, cordial reception has sweetened my lonely path, and if I happen to return to my motherland, to the south, the fire of your benevolence will always glow in my heart."[8]

Aldridge was destined never to return to his motherland. He could visit any remote corner of foreign lands in his travels, but the path to his motherland was denied him for as long as his people were denied a path to freedom.

Aldridge's triumphant tour of Germany, where he spent three years, caused England to remember that he was an English actor, and now as a celebrity, he was invited back to London. In 1850-60s he was offered several engagements there, and he played in Scotland and Ireland too, but he was invariably drawn to the Continent where he received more compassion and attention than in England. Eventually he stopped touring with an English troupe, feeling that it was alien for him to do so; now he preferred to act with Swedish actors in Sweden, with Hungarians in Hungary. In Budapest he was elected an honorable member of the Magyar Drama Conservatory and gave a scholarly speech in English on Shakespeare, Goethe, and Schiller.

In 1858 Aldridge arrived in Riga and performed there with a German troupe. He was received there as a European celebrity. Baltic barons had heard a lot about his enormous success in Germany, but they soon grew disappointed with him. It seemed to them that he acted too "natürlich." His yearning for truth on stage appeared reprehensible to them, insulting to their "enlightened taste," for they were used to

---

8 Ibid., 33-46.

the unnatural acting of pompous tragedians. Aldridge made up his mind to look for new audiences in another country yet unknown to him.

IN ST. PETERSBURG

═ ═ ═ ═ ═ ═ ═ ═ ═ ═ ═ ═ ═ *CB* ═ ═ ═ ═ ═ ═ ═ ═ ═ ═ ═ ═ ═

*I*n November 1858 Aldridge arrived in St. Petersburg and began his performances at the Theater-Circus. This was a time in North America when there was a fierce battle between slave-owners and abolitionists. The abolitionist movement was strengthened by masses of the democratic working class in big cities who fought against major landowners and capitalists simultaneously.[1] In 1852 Harriet Beecher Stowe published *Uncle Tom's Cabin*. The novel was a passionate polemic in support of black slaves and highly critical of slave-owners. Stowe's message spread everywhere as the book was translated into all European languages. It was particularly successful in Russia where its own "negroes" existed—peasant serfs suffering under the yoke of landowners.

1　See D.O. Zaslavsky, *Essays on the History of North American United States, 18th and 19th Centuries* (Moscow: Ogonek, 1931), 75: "The abolitionist movement reminds us of the Russian narodnichestvo (populism movement) in the 1860-70s. The same traits of moral idealism, the same thirst for a fight, for revolutionary activism."

Like North America, Russia was experiencing an intense battle between advocates of serfdom and adherents of peasant freedom. Nikolay Chernyshevsky, a leading revolutionary democrat, published a series of articles exposing attempts by the government and ruling class to place new shackles of economic slavery on the peasants under the guise of "emancipation." In these essays Chernyshevsky emphasized the parallel with the fight of American abolitionists against slave-owners, seeing many similarities with Russia's battle against serfdom, and he could not conceal his heated sympathy for the "radical wing of the party battling against slavery, the so-called party of the abolitionists."[2] Later on, in his novel *What is to Be Done?*, Chernyshevsky had one of his heroes say, "I stand for the illiterate blacks against their civilized owners in the southern states" (Chapter 5, Section 11).

Aldridge's life presents itself as a story that reveals the truth about a black man: his sufferings and his fight for the right to exist and partake in all of humankind's culture. He first became known in St. Petersburg in 1852 after a brief note on him entitled "Negro Actor" appeared in the journal *Pantheon*.[3] And then, on November 10, 1858 [Julian

---

2   See Nikolay Gavrilovich Chernyshevsky, *Polnoe sobranie sochineniy* (Complete Works) (St. Petersburg: M.N. Chernyshevskago, 1906), 8: 371, 503-9; 9:197.

3   A German critic, L. Schuking, in "Negro Actor," *Pantheon* 10, No. 5 (1858): 77, wrote, "The Negro actor is so far removed from the traditions of English theater and the rules of English declamation that we can consider him a truly original phenomenon. Studied effects, like Rachel's, are unknown to him. He masterfully expresses outbursts of passion, cries of anguish, soft tones of tenderness and good-heartedness. He is wonderfully tall, slender and broad-shouldered. His acting and mimicry are striking, and no one has ever better understood

calendar], Aldridge performed there in *Othello*. The huge Theater-Circus was completely sold out. Amongst the spectators there were renowned writers, actors, and scholars. I.I. Panaev wrote in Nekrasov and Chernyshevsky's *Sovremennik* that "When Othello first stepped on stage, after some applause in greeting him, a dead silence ensued, one that is a consequence of anxious curiosity mixed with an involuntary respect for talent that usually forebodes something truly extraordinary. It seemed like a thousand people present there at that moment suddenly held their breath. All the binoculars were focused on the debutant."[4]

The overwhelming majority of the audience who were used to seeing tragedians like Ya. G. Bryansky and V. A. Karatygin as Othello were stunned by Aldridge's acting, which destroyed all the generally accepted criteria of what was "tragic." Genuine bewilderment can be sensed in a review by a critic in *Syn Otechestva*:

> As for the African tragedian's acting, we find ourselves completely baffled by it, for there is so much of the unusual, genuinely savage, and unrestrained element, entirely unknown to us previously, that if we look at his acting from the perspective of our stage craft, it would seem odd and sometimes even awkward, but the actor's talent is so enormous that it quickly demolishes these

---

the character of Othello. Once in Cologne, when he seized Iago by the throat, one spectator screamed: 'It serves the rascal right! Strangle him!' When this man recovered his senses, amid an uproar of laughter, he hurried to leave the theater, saying, 'Well, one can't listen to this actor indifferently.' In comic roles, Aldridge is also very good."

4 I.I. Panaev, "Petersburg Life: Notes of a New Poet," *Sovremennik* (Contemporary) 72, Nos. 11-12 (1858): 260.

routine impressions and carries us into another world, the world of unbridled and wild passions painted by Shakespeare and Shakespeare alone. As Othello, Mr. Aldridge was astonishing—he is a true tiger, and one fears for the artists who play Desdemona and Iago, and after the curtain finally falls, one wants to call for them, at least to make sure that they are still alive.[5]

Amid the bewilderment one can feel in every line of this review, it is really crucial that the author recognizes that the "actor's talent is so enormous that it quickly demolishes these routine impressions" which had become commonplace for Shakespeare's characters on the Russian stage.

A critic writing for *Severnaya Pchela* cited the novelty of Aldridge's approach to Shakespeare's tragedy: "From the very first act, during the speech to the Senate, we saw an extraordinary actor who was trying to earn the audience's sympathy not through shouting and exaggerated outbursts but with simplicity and truthful acting....In Aldridge we saw a truly living Othello, exactly the way the great poet had portrayed him. There was nothing artificial in his acting, just pure nature captured and described not by art but by spirit."[6]

---

5   R. Zotov, "Social Notes," *Syn Otechestva* (Son of the Fatherland) 48 (November 30, 1858): 53.

6   Anon. "Phelka (Little Bee)," *Severnaya Pchela* (Northern Bee) 254 (November 17, 1858): 1070.

Figure 1: Lithograph of Aldridge as Othello

"Simplicity and truthfulness of acting"—this was Aldridge's new contribution to tragedy in St. Petersburg's theater, which was accustomed to the cold recitals and

35

external effects of Karatygin. The lively naturalness of the character and disarming truthfulness of his emotions, coupled with an extraordinary force of personality, were the most striking features instantly observed by his most perceptive Russian spectators. Comparing Aldridge's acting with the usual external rhetorical devices employed by Russian tragic actors, K.I. Zvantsov, a well-known theater critic, distinguished him from other European actors, as well:

> Once Aldridge appeared onstage, it was impossible not to see that he was not one of our kind! The regal nobility of his gait and manners, enchanting diction, perfect knowledge of the stage, *velvety* softness and flexibility of every movement, classical calmness and fullness, but *modest* confidence – all these were the qualities of an actor who had dared to perform in London before people who gave us Shakespeare himself. All these qualities astonish us, the ignoramuses, but in fact could be acquired with enough intelligence and dramatic cleverness. But where are we going to find the living soul with which Aldridge is able to render the deepest designs of the great playwright?

The most striking thing for critics, Zvantsov argued, was that Aldridge was able to combine "two qualities encountered together so rarely: simple, good-nature and a high degree of education....[He is] a son of poor Africa and at the same time the smartest interpreter of Shakespeare!" [7]

From these reviews of Aldridge's first performance, one can see the powerful and multi-sided impression he produced in just one role. Aldridge's first Russian audiences

---

7   K.I. Zvantsov, "Aldridge's Debut in Othello," *Teatralny i Muzikalny Vestnik* (Theatrical and Musical Bulletin) 45 (November 16, 1858): 530-31.

saw an actor of enormous talent and temperament, an artist who refreshed tragedy with his lively truth and exquisite simplicity, and a refined interpreter of one of the world's greatest playwrights.

Two letters written by his spectators are indicative of his huge success in St. Petersburg. One was sent by A.F. Pisemsky to A.N. Maikov on November 24, 1858: "The African tragedian Ira Aldridge is playing Shakespearean roles here, and St. Petersburg is in ecstacy; personally I cannot judge as I don't speak any goddamned English, but, all things considered, it looks to me like this tragedian is passionate but somewhat stupid."[8] Clearly unsympathetic to the Negro actor, Pisemsky still could not conceal the fact that Aldridge had captured the attention of all St. Petersburg.

In the other letter, instead of anything about the actor's "stupidity," we encounter an appeal to go to his performances to see the most profound of all playwrights in an authentic light: "Tomorrow I will tell you what kind of *talent* we saw yesterday in the role of Othello. He is a Negro; he has, of course, many shortcomings, but his talent is tremendous, and certainly I will not see a better Othello for the rest of my life. I advise you not to miss him, in order to understand Shakespeare." This was written in 1858 by V.V. Stasov, a critic who was a fervent admirer of Shakespeare, in a letter to M.A. Balakirev, a composer of remarkable music for Shakespeare's tragedy *King Lear*. When he writes about the "we" who highly appreciated Aldridge, he refers also to L.I. Shestakova, M.I. Glinka's sister.[9]

---

8 A.F. Pisemsky, *Pisma* (Letters) (Moscow: Academy of Sciences, 1936), 128.

9 M.A. Balakirev, *Perepiska M.A. Balakireva s V.V. Stasovym* (Correspondence of M.A. Balakirev with Stassov) (Petrograd: T/D. Lemberg, 1917), 40.

One could cite numerous similar accounts by contemporaries about the powerful artistic impression Aldridge produced in Russia on his first tour, an impression enhanced by the political and social atmosphere in St. Petersburg in 1858. One of the spectators there who saw Aldridge in *Othello* wrote after his first performance: "I am quite convinced that after Aldridge it is impossible to see Othello played by another actor, except perhaps Garrick. In modern history there is a phenomenon that creates whole new experiences of life and thought, namely the emancipation of slaves in North America. It makes enslavement *internal* not just to black people but to any of us."

Remove a layer of self-censorship in these words, and they apparently hint at Russia's millions of white slaves yearning for freedom. "That's why," this spectator continues, "in our time especially, the role of Othello, performed ingeniously by an artist of that people, has a great universal meaning. It is neither Shakespeare nor Aldridge who really interests us at this point but the Negro in general, who has been placed by them face to face with the slave-owning society, and is seen in all his naïve, childlike simplicity, and with

> —a free and open nature,
> That thinks men honest, that but seem to be so,
> And *can* as tenderly be led by the nose,
> As asses are! (Act 1, Scene 3)

Seeing the tamed Othello in front of you trapped by his tamer, seeing a savage lion under the control of an enlightened *European* (this Iago of modern history), against your will you remember the many generations of black people tormented by the whips of American hucksters." In the tragedy *Othello*—in a broad sense—all this was depicted by Shakespeare and shown by Aldridge "so truthfully, so forcefully that we could without exaggeration risk beginning to hate the white characters, at least the Venetians who surround Othello, including maybe even Desdemona herself. It is a pity that she is not black."[10]

Shakespeare's Othello, with his nobility and suffering in Aldridge's interpretation, became a mouthpiece for human dignity and a demonstration of the harsh sufferings of black people who longed for emancipation. Sometimes Aldridge would follow his performance of Othello with a short play, *The Padlock*, in which he took the part of Mungo, a black servant. Aldridge's enemies attacked him for such a frivolity, supposedly an insult to Shakespeare. But Aldridge did have a heartfelt need to portray on stage a real Negro slave, of whose kind there were thousands in North America. In this unpretentious little comedy the great tragedian turned into a superb comedian, but despite his careless gaiety, as the same St. Petersburg spectator recalls, "he produced a grave impression because the role instantly brought to mind some of the saddest scenes from *Uncle Tom's Cabin*." During his later tours in Russia, Aldridge introduced Russian folksongs into the play, and their affinity with the songs of Negro slaves did not seem odd at all; both were songs of slaves, whether white or black.

In artist Ye.F. Yunge's memoir (she was a daughter of renowned sculptor and vice-president of the Academy of the Arts, F.P. Tolstoy) we read: "Aldridge arrived in St. Petersburg in the winter of 1855. We booked several box-seats next to each other and all went to see him in *Othello*, which inspired us so much that after the performance we went to his hotel and waited for him there. Oh Lord, what a

---

10 Zvantsov, *Ira Aldridge*, 17-18.

sight that was! Starov [Shevchenko's friend and Gerzen's admirer. S.D.] kissed his hands, his 'noble black hands'! Shaking with agitation and embarrassment, I could barely translate everything that was being said, the mixture of Russian, French, English, and German words spoken at the same time."[11]

Such were the impressions and feelings stirred by Aldridge amid the advanced circles of St. Petersburg society, in which the emancipation of American slaves and Russian serfs was considered as one of the great tasks of the time. In the same year when Aldridge was impressing audiences there with the truth of his art, Taras G. Shevchenko, after nine years of military service and exile in the Trans-Caspian steppes, returned to the same city. Just as Aldridge had been deprived of an opportunity to perform on stage after the destruction of the Negro Theater in New York, Shevchenko had been for ten years separated from his beloved painting and poetry; Nicholas I, having exiled him to the Southeast, forbade the artist and poet to paint and to write. From his exile Shevchenko wrote to F.P. Tolstoy, "The punishment is terrifying! All my life has been devoted to divine art. And now what? Not to mention the material torture... Albeit with great difficulty, I have denied myself the most vital things. I am happy with what the tsar gives to a soldier. But how can I deny myself the thoughts, the feelings, from this inextinguishable fondness of exquisite art? Oh, please save me, another year, and I will perish."

It was at the house of F.P. Tolstoy (who greatly contributed to retrieving the great Ukrainian poet from exile) that Shevchenko first met Aldridge. The two became bosom friends. As Tolstoy's daughter recalled,

---

11 Yunge, *Vospominaniya*, 166-67.

Oftentimes Aldridge would enter with his quick, energetic step and would instantly inquire: "And the artist?"—this was what he called Shevchenko, as any attempt to pronounce his name would result in him roaring with laughter at his own vain attempts, repeating, "Oh, these difficult Russian surnames!"

Besides being similar in character, these two had much more in common that led to their deep sympathy with one another. One was a serf in his youth, the other belonged to a despised race. Both had experienced a lot of sorrow and bitterness in his life, and both loved their oppressed people dearly. I remember both of them being so deeply moved when I told Aldridge the story of Shevchenko's life, and also translated the tragedian's biography to Shevchenko....Both understood one other so well, both were artists and therefore very observant; both had expressive faces, and Aldridge could express himself perfectly with gestures and mimicry.

Shevchenko decided to draw a portrait of Aldridge....For several minutes one could only hear the squeak of the pencil against the paper, but could Aldridge really sit still? He began to stir, and we yelled at him to sit quietly. He made funny faces. We could not help bursting out laughing. Shevchenko angrily stopped working. Aldridge made a frightened face and sat still for a little while. "May I sing?" he would suddenly ask. "Ah, whatever, let him sing," Shevchenko responded. A touching, sad Negro tune would ensue that would gradually change to a livelier tempo and finish in a mad jig with Aldridge dancing around the studio. Following that, he would perform entire comical scenes from everyday life (he was a superb comedian). Taras Grigorivich, caught up by this merriment, would sing Ukrainian folksongs for him, and then they would start

41

conversing about typical traits of different nations, about the similarity of popular traditions, etc.[12]

Shevchenko sketched a beautiful portrait of Aldridge that is now exhibited in the Tretyakov Gallery. [See frontispiece.]

The celebrated Negro tragedian and great Ukrainian poet thus had profound conversations about the friendship of nations, about the great significance of popular poetry — the art of the workers — for brotherly communication between different peoples, while the interlocutors themselves — a tragedian descended from a persecuted race and a popular poet — were the best examples of the possibility and fruitfulness of such communication, heralding the arrival of those

> Future times
> When nations will forget about their factions
> And will unite in one great family (Pushkin).

---

12 Ibid., 168-70.

Figure 2: Sketch of Aldridge and Taras Shevchenko by L.O. Pasternak

For the main figures of Russia's emancipation movement who fought for the freedom of millions of serfs and for the rights of oppressed nationalities, Aldridge's emergence and his great success were a remarkable tangible argument in defense of human and cultural rights. This was why

Nekrasov and Chernyshevsky's *Sovremennik* devoted a large article to his tour containing a detailed review of his acting in *Othello* and *Merchant of Venice*, the two parts that both in Aldridge's repertoire and in the perception of a Russian spectator acquired a special, emancipatory meaning—that of an ardent manifesto for freeing black slaves and oppressed Jews in tsarist Russia. "Aldridge does not belong to any school. He is simply a great tragedian," the article claimed, which was followed by detailed analysis of his acting, showing that he was a great realist.[13] This side of his talent— his ideological eminence and yearning for the truth of life— made him resemble trends in Russian literature and theater in which ideas of freedom were coupled with the call for realism as an indispensable condition of artistic merit.

The impression produced by Aldridge's acting was so huge that it embraced yet wider circles of Russian society— not only through its artistic power but also through its ideological and social meaningfulness. A highly interesting comment on Aldridge's performances came from a renowned historian M.P. Pogodin (1800-1875). Toward the end of the 1850s Pogodin had moved far away from positions held by *Sovremennik*, and in many aspects he was directly hostile to them. But Pogodin, the son of a serf, had always been an enemy of the gentry's political supremacy in the state as well as a convinced opponent of serfdom. He firmly believed in the purity and strength of the power of common people. This is why Aldridge's emergence stirred him so deeply and inspired his remarkable comment. Shaken by Aldridge, Pogodin wrote,

General opinion places Negroes at the lowest rank among human beings; many think they are inferior, both morally

---

13 Panaev, "Petersburg Life," 274.

and intellectually, to their white counterparts of blue blood, but just look at Aldridge: here he is, an African, with a swarthy face, with black skin, with curly hair, broad nostrils, and guttural speech. He does not attract our attention by any refined forms that we are accustomed to: external beauty does not help him produce a favorable impression on any of us. More than that, he speaks a foreign, alien language, but such is the power of his soul, such is the might of his art, that you submit to him from the very first minute; you understand whatever he says, you guess everything he feels, you seem to hear his every heartbeat, and with this magician you go through all the stages of human passions, experience all the degrees of heat, and reach a point where you catch your breath, where mercury freezes. Love, hatred, anger, affection, timidity, simplemindedness, and rage are expressed by this Negro with equal astounding power. All the tiniest, most minute details of human emotions recorded by the foremost connoisseur and observer of human nature, Shakespeare, are rendered with stunning accuracy. And one can detect in the very depths of every delighted spectator's heart an understanding that under Aldridge's swarthy skin there beats the same heart that beats in the breasts of all other people, his stifled chest emits the same heavy sighs, his black body shivers in pain just like a white one does. Negroes feel, suffer, rejoice, and moan in exactly the same way white people do. Circumstances and history for some yet unclear reasons have brought them to their current condition, humiliated and unhappy. But such circumstances and history also control the whites. The whites also may find themselves in the mire, drowning in dirt, and blackened in heart and soul. The whites, history teaches us, can also become stupid, their spirit weakened, their speech inarticulate; their sense of shame and honor abandons them; divine fire disappears from their eyes; a brutish smile appears on their lips; and a man turns into an animal, not under the whip, cane or rod, but due to fear that he may find himself under one....It is absurd to think that such a condition is natural for a black or white person; it is absurd to think that in order to improve, ennoble, or reinvigorate himself, a black or white person only needs a period of time, short or long....

What a delightful spectacle it is for a man to see the whole race, white or black, awakened to human life! Such were the thoughts stirred in me by the African Negro's acting, but acting in what exactly, do you think? In the farce *The Padlock*. When the cruel master threatens the timid slave with a cane, I noticed just one spasmodic movement of his back, his shoulder, and I myself began trembling with my whole body; I saw the entire tribe's history in my imagination.[14]

It is unlikely that Pogodin could only imagine the *black* tribe's history. Censor Boris Fyodorov had corrected the proofs of the article on Aldridge; he realized that Pogodin's hot-blooded essay spoke not just about African slaves but also about white serfs yearning for freedom and possessing all the rights for development and culture. Pogodin did not even try to conceal it as he spoke about the "delightful spectacle of seeing the whole race, white or black, awakened to human life." The whip raised by the "cruel master over the timid slave" was in his eyes the same lash that some kind of a Sobakevich would use to slash the back of a Tula or Orel muzhik (peasant).

It would be incredible if in St. Petersburg, the capital of a serf empire, there had been no Aldridge adversaries. There were some. They managed to have Macbeth banned from his tour. They harshly attacked the Negro who dared to perform

---

14 Nikolay Platonovich Barsukov, *Zhizn' i trudy M.P. Pogodina* (Pogodin's Life and Works) (St. Petersburg: M.M. Stasiulevich, 1902), 16:192-96.

in the tsar's capital. Like Pogodin's censor, they realized what political parallels Aldridge drew by the mere fact of his existence, and these serfdom advocates strove to present the black actor's performance as the absurd raging of a savage that was not a worthy spectacle for a white, noble audience. It was these Aldridge enemies that I.I. Panaev had in mind when he wrote in *Sovremennik*: "It is not his African appearance, as these gentlemen believe, not his savage physiognomy, not his voice that resembles jackals' howling, not the greenish whites of his eyes (I am using their expressions), and not his rages that win the audience to his side, but that inner flame, which reveals him to be a first-rate tragedian."[15]

Three years later, serfdom advocates in Moscow began a defamation campaign against Aldridge. But their vicious hissing was drowned out by a chorus of wide recognition of the wonderful actor. He was received warmly and cordially by the best representatives of Russia's literature, theater, and society. Aldridge enjoyed exceptional success in an area in which an actor usually finds it hard to be successful: among fellow actors. His performances were attended by actors who took them as lessons in stagecraft. Gogol's famous associate I.I. Sosnitsky, the creator of the role of the Mayor in *The Inspector General*, wrote to actress A.M. Chitau about Aldridge, saying, "Never in my life have I ever seen such talent, and I never even dreamed of one like that. It is really astonishing to what heights a genius can reach."[16] The entire dramatic troupe of the Imperial Theater of St. Petersburg

---

15 Panaev, "Petersburg Life," 274. In January 1859 Panaev noted Aldridge's departure.

16 Sergei L'vovich Bertenson, *Ded russkoi stseny* (Grandfather of the Russian Stage) (Petrograd: Mitjurnikov in Komm., 1916), 147.

united to honor him, with the sole exception of V.V. Samoilov, who saw in Aldridge a rival for Shakespearean parts.[17] All the other members of the troupe, as a sign of their sincere friendship with the touring tragedian, posed for a group photograph with Aldridge.

The affection for Aldridge was particularly clear on his benefit night, when he played Othello. His success was remarkable. An experienced chronicler said, "Upon his arrival on stage, the artist was greeted with a triple explosion of delight, in which it was impossible to distinguish between ovations, shouts, stamping, or banging on the chairs; I had never heard such a deafening hurricane here since the visit of [Pauline] Viardot."[18] Pogodin, who was also present at the benefit, wrote, "In some parts of *Othello* he seemed to even surpass himself. The delight was indescribable. Men and women, sitting in box seats and

---

17 Samoilov instigated an article [by R. Zotov] in *Syn Otechestva* (Son of the Fatherland) 48 (November 30, 1858): 1543, hailing him as "our actor of genius whose Lear is superior to that of the touring African tragedian." This brought a rebuttal from an anonymous author in *Severnaya Pchela* (Northern Bee) 278 (December 17, 1858): 1165, arguing that the journalist in *Syn Otechestva* certainly exaggerated and was "too carried away when he suggested that our local actor is better than Aldridge. Lots of readers found his outburst rather peculiar." In response, Zotov continued to claim Samoilov's superiority, treating it as an essentially a racial matter: white being better than black. He even noted that Aldridge himself had admitted that Samoilov was better than himself as Lear. [See *Syn Otechestva* 1 (January 4, 1859): 4.] Today we are unable to verify this claim.

18 K.I. Zvantsov, "Mr. Ira Aldridge's Benefit," *Teatralny i Muzikalny Vestnik* (Theatrical and Musical Bulletin) 51 (December 28, 1858): 602.

chairs, were up on their feet waving their hats and headscarves and shouting. The bursts of applause followed one another."[19]

At the end of the performance Aldridge was treated to a rare celebration in his honor—it was done by the actors. The oldest actor of the St. Petersburg stage, the famous I.I. Sosnitsky, presented Aldridge with a wonderful painting of Shakespeare surrounded by Thalia, Melpomene and Calliope. The painting was inscribed in English and Russian: "To Ira Aldridge from Russian Actors." The inscription was followed by a poem by actor P.I. Grigoriev:

Through your wit, talent and labor
You explained the great Shakespeare to the Russians!
We will never forget from now on
Othello, Shylock and Lear!

The painting was signed by all the actors of the Alexandrinsky Theater, headed by Sosnitsky and Martynov. "Together with the painting," Pogodin tells us, "Sosnitsky gave him a laurel garland with a red ribbon and a wide golden ring that had the following inscribed: 'To Ira Aldridge, a great interpreter of immortal Shakespeare, from Russian actors, St. Petersburg, 1858.' Aldridge shook his hand, clearly touched, and thanked the audience. He was covered in wreaths and bouquets; the storm of applause was very loud and prolonged." This was more than a theatrical triumph of one actor. This was a demonstration of social feelings and emancipatory strivings. This is why Pogodin finished his report about Aldridge's benefit with the following meaningful statement: "Between the Hyperboreans and the Negro, some touching mutual

---

19 Barsukov, *Zhizn' i trudy M.P. Pogodina*, 16:197.

sympathy, a cordial union, ensued. Yes, we are all human, we are all brothers, born with the same labor pains, experiencing the same sorrows and joys."[20]

The unusual reception given to Aldridge in St. Petersburg produced the most decisive impact on his life. From then on, he began considering Russia his second motherland, and of the remaining years of his life (1859-1867), there were just two (1860 and 1863) when he did not visit Russia. In 1867, as he was traveling to St. Petersburg again, Aldridge fell ill and died in Lodz, i.e., within the borders of the Russian Empire.

---

20 Ibid. Cf. Zvantsov, "Mr. Ira Aldridge's Benefit," 602-3.

ALDRIDGE AS KING LEAR

═ ═ ═ ═ ═ ═ ═ ═ ═ ═ ═ ═ ═ ℭℨ ═ ═ ═ ═ ═ ═ ═ ═ ═ ═ ═ ═ ═

*I*n his early youth Aldridge began his acting career playing Romeo. He learned stagecraft from Shakespeare's tragedies. Having achieved wide renown, he gave all his energy to creating Shakespearean characters.

A.N. Bazhenov, a remarkable theater critic of the 1860s and an ardent proponent of Shakespeare's repertoire in the Russian theater, saw Aldridge several times at the Maly Theater in Moscow, and then wrote:

> I eagerly went to see Aldridge's performances and learned so much from them; it was more than you can learn in a whole year. Those evenings were definitely the best time I have ever had in a theater. It was a festival of genuinely artistic representations of Shakespeare's finest creations; before me passed, one after the other, four beautifully interpreted, completely living characters that will never be erased from my memory.[1]

---

1 Aleksandr Nikolaevich Bazhenov, *Sochinenia i Perevod* (Collected Works and Translations) (Moscow: Tip Kosogorova, 1869), 1:181.

Aldridge's fondness for Shakespeare corresponded with his deep knowledge of this great playwright. His critics were stunned by his exceptional understanding of Shakespeare.

> Just like a lover not being able to take his eyes away from the object of his love, as if he were afraid to miss something, Aldridge was in awe of Shakespeare's characters and analyzed them with extraordinary sharpness without missing a single minute trait and, where necessary, beautifully read between the lines. Having a profound knowledge of this connoisseur of life and the human heart, Aldridge understood the consistency and internal necessity with which Shakespeare developed action in all his works, the way one thing was always derived from another, and how sometimes even an insignificant detail left without notice could render the following sequence absolutely unclear. Therefore Aldridge was afraid that his spectators too might miss something from the Shakespeare he transmitted to them. He thoroughly, meticulously refined every line in his role; as he was playing it, he was also interpreting it.[2]

Before Aldridge's arrival there also were talented performers of Shakespeare in Russia: Pavel S. Mochalov, whose repertoire included six Shakespearean roles, instantly comes to mind. But in Russia there had never been an actor who would dedicate all his talent, thought, and feeling to only Shakespeare and nothing else. Aldridge was not simply an actor performing in Shakespeare's tragedies; he was a Shakespeare enthusiast, a passionate proponent of his plays. Aldridge's tours were extremely timely: Russian actors were eager to learn the real art of playing Shakespeare from him; spectators were ready to absorb the greatness of the playwright's thoughts and feelings. Of all his tragedies, only

---

2   Ibid., 1:181-83.

Hamlet had been widely popular in Russia, thanks largely to Mochalov's genius in creating the unforgettable character of the Prince of Denmark, and to N.A. Polevoy's translation and adaptation of the play, which had appealed to public taste in the 1830-40s due to its romantic melodramatics. Of all the other tragedies, Russian audiences were less familiar with *Othello* and *King Lear*, had a little better knowledge of *The Merchant of Venice*, and had never before seen *Macbeth*. But after the deaths of Mochalov in 1848 and Vasilly A. Karatygin in 1853, even those portions of the Shakespearean repertoire were clearly depleted. Provincial theaters kept on playing *Hamlet* in Mochalov's version, and sometimes *Othello* occasionally. Even at Moscow's Maly Theater, this citadel of Shakespeareanism in Russia, his tragedies were staged very seldom.

It was then that Aldridge began his Shakespearean journey around Russia that lasted nine years. During this time he played King Lear, Macbeth, Shylock, Richard III, and Othello, as well as only one small non-Shakespearean role—that of Mungo, the mulatto in Isaac Bickerstaff's comedy *The Padlock*. Aldridge performed as Richard III most rarely and apparently had the least success in that role, judging from the silence in the press on his performances of this character. The only review appeared in Odessa in 1866 and was so belligerent that it failed to offer an objective evaluation of his performance. The critic's main focus was on the fact that Aldridge's treatment of the character was different from the one given by the well-known critic Rötscher.[3]

---

3   S.T. Gertso-Vinogradskii, "Mr. Ira Aldridge in the role 'Richard III,'" *Odesskii Vestnik* (Odessa Bulletin) 30 (1866): 95-96. [Signed N.N.]

Between the work of an actor and that of a playwright, composer or painter there is a huge difference. It lies in the fact that a work of art created by the latter can exist only as a material phenomenon. A Surikov painting, a Beethoven symphony, Pushkin's *Eugene Onegin*—all exist although their creators have long been dead. If we do not write another single word about Pushkin's *Onegin* or about Antokolsky's sculptures, they will still exist for the reader and spectator regardless. But the character of Hamlet created by Mochalov, or the character of the Mayor created by Shchepkin, cease their existence when the actor stops performing and leaves the stage. Someone who writes about Surikov does not have to restore his whole painting *Boyarina Morozova* in the reader's memory; it is enough for him to refer to the actual painting or to show a good reproduction of it. Someone writing on Beethoven does not have to recount his symphony in words; he can send readers to its score or to its piano transposition. An author of a book about an actor is deprived of such an opportunity. Meanwhile, in order to correctly interpret Aldridge's legacy, we need to transform ourselves for a few moments from the *readers* of 1940 to *spectators* of the 1860s, who actually *saw* him act as Shakespeare's characters. An art historian or archeologist can use only fragments to reconstruct the whole statue. Let us try to use the fragments of the audience's impressions to reconstruct Aldridge's Shakespearean characters.

One of the most difficult characters for an actor in all of Shakespeare is King Lear. The excellence of Aldridge's performance as Lear was unanimously recognized in Russia. At one point Goethe attacked Shakespeare for the arbitrariness of Lear's actions at the beginning of the play, and Leo Tolstoy criticized the development of the tragedy that ensued as unnatural. One of the most difficult tasks faced by an actor playing Lear is to find an explanation for the king's decisions within the character himself and present it in a convincing way so that all the subsequent actions would be conditioned by it. All the misfortunes that befall Lear begin with his decision to abdicate and divide the kingdom between his daughters. But from where does he get this thought about dividing the kingdom? From a sudden whim—this is the answer given by some of Lear's interpreters onstage. From a weary satiety of power—this is what some others say. From his emerging psychiatric disorder, which is not yet discernible to outsiders—some others claim.

Aldridge's opinion is that it comes from Lear's limitless fatherly love. This love is so sublime and so humane that for its sake Lear is ready to give up royal power and become just a man, just a father. In Aldridge's interpretation, the more Lear is full of love for his children, the more he trusts them unconditionally. The scene of dividing the kingdom, that always stumped critics and was dubbed "absurd" by Goethe, acquires a deep meaning for Aldridge. Lear wants to step down forever from his throne due to his love for his children. "This is not a regal whim, but a father's desire to recognize the independence of his adult daughters who have the full right to have it."[4]

Fondness of his children is, according to Aldridge, only one aspect of the love that Lear conceals under the surface of his royal grandeur. Lear's good nature is a spiritual trait that sets the pace for everything. "Minutes of hot temper, unjust anger, and horrible curses take place in Lear due to his highly-developed sense of justice and good. This character

---

4   Bazhenov, *Sochinenia i Perevod*, 1:184.

trait was superbly understood by Aldridge."[5] Lear believes that everything in the world follows the laws of good, and his warm love for his daughters and his separation of the kingdom between them is one of the consequences of this conviction. A king alienated from real life through the exceptionality of his position, Lear does not know that life is ruled by savage, brutal laws. Lear the man does not know people because Lear the king only knew his courtiers.

And here the bitter tragedy of Lear begins: having ceased being a king and now just a common man, he suffers one disappointment after another, one disaster after another; his life becomes full of evil and violence previously shielded from him by the impenetrable walls of the royal castle. He is shaken to the point of insanity, he is breaking down in his loneliness and reaches out to all the meek, wretched, and persecuted. The king thus dies in him, and a human being is born in intense pain. This is, in Aldridge's wonderful interpretation, Lear's tragic path from a king with unlimited power to a man who finds respite from innumerable misfortunes and bitter homelessness only in death. Aldridge treats this path with strict consistency and precise correspondence to the logic of Lear's behavior that lies in the character as it was created by Shakespeare. "Temperament, soul, habits, movements," one of the contemporaries tells us, "all the sides of the character came alive in Mr. Aldridge's creation....It is a shame even to discuss certain scenes and details: everything was great."[6] Yet contemporaries still speak about "certain scenes" in which the special power and fascinating truth of Aldridge's conception was found:

---

5 N.S. Nazarov, "Aldridge in *King Lear*," *Russkii Vestnik* (Russian Bulletin) 42 (1862): 25. [Signed N.N.]

6 K.I. Zvantsov, *"King Lear,"* *Teatralny i Muzikalny Vestnik* (Theatrical and Musical Bulletin) 48 (December 7, 1858): 565.

At the beginning of the first act, during the magnanimous division of the kingdom between the elder daughters, he showed extraordinary good nature, even if to the detriment of his regal grandeur. You should have seen him passing his finger over the map delineating the borders of both sisters' estates; you should have seen him reproaching Cordelia for her alleged insensitiveness and how he was ready to forgive her and equalize her with the others at her first word that would show him that she loved him not less than the other sisters. How good-naturedly and tenderly he looks on at the beginning of the scene at his court, at its glitter and splendor! How he wallows in this glitter and splendor! This is how we see the tsar accustomed to reverence and luxury, prone to make mistakes but always conscientious and good-natured. He is confident that everyone is devoted to him sincerely and unconditionally, and he is happy to hear the expressions of this devotion. Weary of his old age and power, he generously endows his daughters, passes the reins of government over to them, and is convinced that his good deeds, his longstanding just and mild rule would secure him being enveloped by honor and love till the end of his days—both as a monarch and a father who had deserved it for all his love and kindness. His good-natured blindness is obvious in Aldridge's acting and is striking in its wonderful artistic expression.[7]

The scene at Goneril's estate (Act 1, Scene 4) features the first bitter disappointment of the unfortunate king:

Aldridge's performance in this scene is among the best in the play. Ingratitude—this is what struck Lear and later caused his insanity.

---

7   Ibid.

Aldridge acted out the whole scene with astonishing artistry. First, he expressed complete bewilderment: he seemed not to understand what was going on around him; he couldn't believe that this was actually happening to him. But later, when this had become obvious, he was desperate beyond any limits: he was yelling, moaning, losing his temper, rushing to everyone seeking protection for his broken feelings and violated justice. Those around him do not understand him: some are happy with his humiliation; others feel sorry for him, are devoted to him but think that his misfortune was naturally caused by his own imprudence. Lear addresses the highest forces of nature:

Hear, Nature, hear! Dear goddess, hear!
Suspend thy purpose, if thou didst intend
To make this creature fruitful!
Into her womb convey sterility!

This monologue, a monologue of curses, is pronounced by Aldridge on bended knees, and one cannot possibly describe the striking effect his voice, mimicry, and gestures produce upon his spectators. The decrepit old man, suddenly struck by grief, kneels on one knee, with his royal cape and staff thrown far away from him, not so much in words but in heartbreaking moans, begins to heap the unbearably painful emotions he is experiencing himself on his daughter. He shouts, he shrieks, he chokes on his own words, he loses breath; it is obvious that everything inside him has been broken and his soul is filled with chaos and suffering. Here the art of the actor had to merge with real feeling, and Aldridge seemingly merged with Lear; one cannot forget this decrepit, desperate old man's voice, this look full of agony and indignation. The actor's mimicry was striking, despite the fact that the lower part of his face was hidden behind a broad gray beard.

In Act 2 the situation partly repeats itself but here Lear's crucial moment is his defense of Kent (Scene 4). In the whole scene, just as before, it is not the lofty and horrible anger of a strong, hardhearted man that dominates but again the frenzy of a kind man who has lost his equanimity and no longer is in control of his actions. Thanks to Aldridge's acting we see quite clearly that such a man inevitably has to end up going crazy.

But Lear's insanity is also a combination of his good nature and frenzy. In the midst of the tempest and thunderstorm, in the midst of his gloomiest despair and half-insane thoughts about life, when he is already conscious of his mistake and his guilt concerning Cordelia, Lear meets with Edgar who appears first as *poor Tom*. The king seemingly sees a brother in him, a fellow human being who, just like himself, has been thrown out of his mundane groove, shaken by his grief and misfortunes. Suddenly he feels enormous sympathy towards him and with limitless good-nature sits down next to him on bare earth to sort out straws. The venerable old man turns into a small child. The malice and injustice of the world have brought together these two opposite extremes: a king and a holy fool. Filled with internal agony, Lear is alien to the whole world and finds his only kin in poor Tom the holy fool; the latter is also suffering and alienated from the world. We know that Lear is facing not a real Tom but Edgar who appears as him. But Edgar too has been cast out by the world and his father; he is also a victim of injustice and ingratitude. One cannot watch Aldridge without tears as he embraces Edgar in his rags, having torn apart his own clothes and having sorted straws with him.[8]

---

8   Nazarov, "Aldridge in *King Lear*," 25-26.

At this grave hour, *King* Lear's kindness transforms into a new, broader feeling—the brotherhood of the *human being* Lear with all the miserable and wretched:

> Poor naked wretches, whereso'er you are,
> That bide the pelting of this pitiless storm,
> How shall your houseless heads and unfed sides,
> Your looped and windowed raggedness, defend you
> From seasons such as these? O, I have ta'en
> Too little care of this! Take physic, pomp;
> Expose thyself to feel what wretches feel….(Act 3, Scene 4)

In these words one finds the main leitmotif of the whole Edgar scene in the interpretation and performance offered by Aldridge.

In Act 4, Scene 6, Aldridge was stunning as he "appeared as a miserable, ragged Lear with a straw wreath and a straw scepter in his trembling hands, with statesmanlike imperturbability in his foggy gaze, as he is already unable to distinguish his friends and loyal subjects. Lear's words had a magic effect when blind Gloucester, having recognized his voice, asks whether he is the king:

> Ay, every inch a king.
> When I do stare, see how the subject quakes."[9] (Act 4,
> Scene 5)

"In the insanity scene Aldridge was really touching but at the same time so imposing that one would feel compassion toward him, not pity."[10]

---

9   Zvantsov, "*King Lear*," 565

10 Yunge, *Vospominaniya*, 170.

Figure 3: Photo of Aldridge as King Lear

"The famous scene of the exhausted king in Cordelia's tent was performed in such a way that only stones could contain their tears. One cannot imagine the tender feeling of fondness, the concentrated bliss, that old man's half-conscious shame portrayed by Aldridge that fill his utterances such as the following one:

> Pray, do not mock me:
> I am a very foolish fond old man,
> Fourscore and upward, not an hour more nor less;
> And, to deal plainly,
> I fear I am not in my perfect mind. (Act 4, Scene 6)

Or this one:

> Pray you now, forget and forgive: I am old and foolish."[11]

"We are facing a half-dead Lear who is holding on to life only through his love for Cordelia, a love that gets only stronger and deeper when it is experienced in the time of sufferings and insanity. After his mind came back to him, thanks to his daughter's care, and he recognized Cordelia, he can no longer exist without her; he looks for her everywhere, he clings on to her, he cannot make a step without his Cordelia."[12]

"It all culminated in the last scene when Lear with widely open eyes and distorted face runs into the stage carrying dead Cordelia in his arms. He seems to be about to throw her against the floor and destroy everything around him, but then his gaze falls on her face, and the old man's face softens, he sits on the floor and presses his daughter

---

11 Zvantsov, "King Lear," 565.
12 Nazarov, "Aldridge in King Lear," 27.

against his chest, nurses and caresses her, and his whole self is transformed into love and grief."[13]

> You see a stamp of death on his face already....Shakespeare's amazing mind in the actor's artistic performance is striking in its new astonishment. Obviously Lear is not going to live for a long time in this world; it is all a matter of minutes now. Death is already choking him; he asks for his coat to be unbuttoned; he is clearly dying, but to the last minute he still hopes that Cordelia will revive. Kent and others surround him, trying to entertain him; he does not see anyone, nor does he recognize anyone; he does not believe that Kent is alive, even though he talks to him; he is completely attached to the corpse of his daughter; he is looking for any glimmer of life in her; it seems to him Cordelia is still alive, that her lips are moving, and he appeals to the others to make sure he is right: 'Look there, look there!' With these words Lear dies. The king's death is played simply and strikingly by Aldridge: quietly, with a slight smile on his lips, he whispers his last words, moving his fingers convulsively, then he throws himself onto the arms of those around him, and his eyes dim—no convulsions, no death agony, nothing. Even those around him do not yet believe that he is dead, but you already are scared and catching your breath; there is a stiff corpse before you now that was alive only a minute ago.[14]

If at the beginning of the tragedy one could repeat the following words about Aldridge's Lear: "Ay, every inch a king," then toward the end one should change them into "human, every inch human—in his reason, in his heart."

---

13 Yunge, *Vospominaniya*, 170.
14 Nazarov, "Aldridge in *King Lear*," 27.

The impression Aldridge made upon Russian actors and spectators as King Lear, and the enormous artistic truth displayed in his acting, will become clear if we juxtapose Aldridge's Lear with Lear played by Vasili V. Samoilov. In a special article on "Mr. Samoilov and Mr. Ira Aldridge in the Role of Shakespeare's Lear" we read,

> Samoilov presented *himself,* but never presented Lear. From the very beginning to the end of the play he presents a man who acts according to whims, and in his despair goes mad. But he did not express the stormy passions and strong personality of this senile man who is driven to lunacy from spiritual anger, from the tortures of a father's heart....It seemed to us that his Lear did not fully feel what he said and did.
>
> A few days later we saw Ira Aldridge play the same part....Aldridge was the true Lear, and in the most powerful Shakespearean scenes he is enchanting....Here is Lear, the real Lear as we imagined him to be!

Pointing to a number of unfavorable conditions in which Aldridge had to perform (bad troupe, foreign language, abridged text, etc.), the author notes that "All of this did not prevent Aldridge from enthralling us, from bringing us to pity, to terror, to tears....What a great actor Mr. Aldridge is!"[15]

The critic Bazhenov described Samoilov as Lear in the following way: "We saw that the actor studies the role and knows it, but he has not felt it deeply and is not living it."[16] Aldridge was a direct opposite of Samoilov, and Pogodin saw this very well when he wrote, "Aldridge is amazing in

---

15 K.A. Polevoi, "Theatrical Chronicle: Mr. Samoilov and Mr. Ira Aldridge in the Role of Shakespeare's Lear," *Severnaya Pchela* (Northern Bee) 287 (December 31, 1858): 1201-2 [Signed K.P.].

16 Bazhenov, *Sochinenia i Perevod,* 1:287.

Othello, Lear, Shylock....No, these are not the roles he studied: these are Othello, Lear, Shylock themselves. You will see how a feeling is born in his heart, how words are found in his mind."[17] With these words Pogodin argued that Aldridge had brought to the Russian stage something that had been missing since Mochalov's death: the living truth of feelings and the genuineness of the breath of life.

---

17 Barsukov, *Zhizn' i trudy M.P. Pogodina*, 195.

ALDRIDGE AS SHYLOCK AND MACBETH

══════════════ ∞ ══════════════

*A*ldridge included only four acts from *The Merchant of Venice* in his performances, concentrating solely on the tragedy of Shylock the Jew and not on the drama of commercial and everyday troubles of Antonio, the unfortunate "Venetian merchant." Just as in *King Lear*, Aldridge stunned his Russian audiences with the novelty of his interpretation of Shylock. Critics noticed this instantly:

> Other actors whom we had seen before presented Shylock as a heartless money-grabber, a huckster, ridiculous in his demands, insatiable greed, and impudence—in other words, they showed him as a caricature. But Aldridge understood this character differently. He represents Shylock as greedy and covetous, yet at the same time proud and self-righteous, filled with thoughts of revenge, hatred, and malice toward Christians, the enemies of his kith and kin. [1]

Aldridge deeply understood this character and played him as an "oppressed, despised Jew, whose daughter has

---

1   Anon. "Phelka (Little Bee)," *Severnaya Pchela* (Northern Bee) 259 (November 24, 1858): 1089.

been stolen away after having been taught to rob him, and who lends Antonio money without interest, yet is deprived of the right to take revenge for all the hatred and unrelenting insults he experiences," a Jew who "finally, is made on penalty of death to betray the faith of his forefathers and bequeath his estate to his daughter's captor."[2] But he loves his daughter passionately—not less than Lear does his daughters, but with a different type of love: he loves her as if she were an irreplaceable treasure, one he is afraid to lose.

The scene with Jessica in Act 2, Scene 5, as performed by Aldridge, was one of the best in the whole play. Getting ready for going to supper with the "Christian spendthrift" (Bassanio), Shylock feasts his eyes on his daughter. "He fondles her tenderly, kisses her, gives her a jewelry ring, and gives her a long loving look as he leaves."[3]

> It may appear to many that Aldridge has his Shylock show too much love for his Jessica in Act 2, Scene 5; is he not too arbitrary in his treatment of Shakespeare in this case? This love is, first of all, shown to prepare for the scene of despair after the daughter's flight in Act 3, Scene 1. Secondly, it explains the care with which he forbids Jessica to lean out the window or go outside, and orders her to tightly lock all the doors. He cherishes her like a precious jewel, guarding her from everything to which he himself

---

2   K.I. Zvantsov, "2. *The Merchant of Venice*," *Teatralny i Muzikalny Vestnik* (Theatrical and Musical Bulletin) 46 (November 23, 1858.): 545-46.

3   A.P. Lensky, in "Notes of an Actor," *Artist* 36 (1894): 100, objected to the scene in which Aldridge, as Shylock, demonstrates his love for his daughter. Lensky wrote, "All this is done to make Shylock sympathetic in the eyes of the audience and enable Aldridge to receive more applause." While the initial hypothesis is justifiable, the latter one has no foundation.

feels revulsion. He loves her with a most jealous kind of love.[4]

This love for a daughter who cheats him for the sake of a Christian lover aggravates and takes to the limit the tragedy of Shylock—the tragedy of a Jew. Shylock has lots of money, but he has even more insults and abuse; he carries all the grief and sorrow of the Jewish people inside himself. And when his daughter is abducted, Shylock finds himself forced into the abyss of hopeless loneliness. His active, vibrant nature is filled not with anger but with a desire for revenge.

In Shylock Aldridge created superbly a medieval Jew— rich, proud, but constantly abused and humiliated by the Christian society around him. How good he was in the scene when he was hesitant to cut off a slice of meat from a Christian! How gleefully and viciously his eyes flashed when he almost made up his mind to take revenge for all his misfortunes on this Christian. The last scene is no less remarkable. The Christians enumerate to Shylock all the punishments that he must suffer for his attempt at murdering a citizen of Venice. However harsh these punishments, Aldridge/Shylock, as he listens to the sentence being read by the judge, does not become fully despondent except when told that he has to convert to Christianity; then he begins shivering as though he had fever, and a long shriek comes from his chest that has nothing to do with articulate human speech. After that, as one of those standing in front of him, a man whose faith he hates, seizes him by his coat, all the contempt and disgust for Christianity is reflected in the Jew, and Aldridge creates a splendid mute scene out of it. The Jew has forgotten that he is in the room, forgets that he belongs to the oppressed, powerless tribe that is never forgiven for anything; he forcefully snatches his garment out of the

---

4   Bazhenov, *Sochinenia i Perevod*, 1:184.

defiling hand of the Christian, then produces his handkerchief and thoroughly cleans the spot fouled by the evil touch, looks at the handkerchief with disgust and abhorrence, and finally tosses it indignantly at the Christian, bursts into tears, and leaves.[5]

For ending the tragedy with this striking mute scene that is totally absent from Shakespeare's text, Aldridge was attacked both by his enemies and even by some of his friends. K.I. Zvantsov, an ardent supporter, wrote, "Having elevated Shylock to the heights of a highly tragic character, Aldridge is of course entitled to play only the four acts— simply because Shylock does not appear on stage in the fifth." But, he argues, "if the drama is founded on this, then he should make up some other tragic finale, perhaps by having Shylock executed, thereby returning him to the status of a victim of appalling injustice."[6]

A critic from the reactionary *Nashe Vremya*, unhappy with the treatment of Shylock and especially with Aldridge's ending of the drama, reluctantly agreed that "everything was performed well," but then attacked him by asserting, "It was more of a pantomime ballet that spoiled the drama, depriving the action of its intensity."[7] But Aldridge knew what he was doing when he finished the play with the mute scene. He did not have to make things up and add an artificial finale to Act 4. The only conclusion of the Shylock's drama for him was drawn from deep within his own emotions. In order to portray the tragedy of a Jew downtrodden and powerless to take revenge for the abuse

---

5   B. Almazov, "Aldridge on the Moscow Stage," *Russkii Vestnik* (Russian Bulletin) 41 (1862): 12.

6   Zvantsov, "2. *The Merchant of Venice*," 545-46.

7   Anon. "Ira Aldridge as Shylock," *Nashe Vremya* (Our Time) 210 (September 30, 1862): 839.

he suffered, one did not need words. Shylock in any case could not have anything to say, as he was surrounded by enemies and expected further acts of violence to be inflicted on him.

At the court Shylock is disgraced, ruined, and sentenced to multiple punishments. But even this is not enough: he is forced to convert to Christianity. In Shakespeare's text, Shylock leaves upon hearing the disgusting parting words from "Christian" Graziano:

> In christening shalt thou have two godfathers.
> Had I been judge, thou shouldst have had ten more,
> To bring thee to the gallows, not to the font. (Act 4, Scene 1)

To this Shylock could only respond in the way Aldridge showed it: with the great wrath of silence, a mute outburst of contemptuous loathing toward the sneering executioners. Of the power of the tragic impression produced by Aldridge in this speechless finale, a contemporary writes: "His acting is remarkable for its effects, both loud and quiet: he shocks the spectator with the former and makes further impression with the latter. And even his silence is eloquent. The last scene before the court he plays almost without words but with captivating eloquence. One can say that he reads Shakespeare between the lines."[8]

In Shylock Aldridge achieved complete reincarnation. "Aldridge makes himself up superbly," Zvantsov says. "One could recognize only his voice. Gestures, gait, manners, even height—everything was changed: a thoroughly whitened face, a large bald spot, black sidelocks and a pointed beard, a glued-on hooked nose, and a naturally large mouth with thick lips and protruding chin. All these features added strikingly to the traits of the Israeli tribe and unwittingly

---

8   Anon. "Phelka (Little Bee)," 259:1089.

transported us into Shakespeare's dramatic sphere." But Aldridge made one mistake here, in Zvantsov's opinion: "He resembled a poetic rendering of Ahasuerus, the so-called Eternal Jew, rather than the Jew Shylock."[9]

If this were so, then certainly in this "mistake" Aldridge demonstrated his creative genius. As in *Othello*, when playing a Venetian Moor, he was able to give a generalized portrait of a suffering slave who yearned for and deserved freedom, so in Shylock did Aldridge give a completely real representation of a Venetian Jew, while simultaneously creating a profound generalized image of a man persecuted and driven to despair.

Russian spectators of the late 1850s were perceptive enough to capture the autobiographical dimension of Aldridge's interpretation of Shylock: "Ira Aldridge is a mulatto, born in America, and he deeply feels the insults being inflicted on colored people by whites in the New World. In Shylock he sees not just a Jew but a human being afflicted by hatred of his fellow human beings, and expresses this feeling with amazing truth and passion."[10]

Aldridge considered Macbeth his best role. In St. Petersburg, due to censorship, he was unable to perform it. He first played Macbeth in Moscow in 1862 and afterwards in the provinces. Fearing censorship, he was forced to stage it in some places without posting any playbills. Macbeth was his crowning achievement. It was in this role that his creative genius manifested itself to the greatest degree. In *Macbeth* Aldridge gave a meticulous and thoughtful performance.

---

9   Zvantsov, "2. *The Merchant of Venice*," 545-46.
10   Anon. "Phelka (Little Bee)," 259:1089.

Had it not been for this, so to speak, complete realization of his role, how could Aldridge show us with such clarity Macbeth as a son of his time, a time in which he asked himself, "If a murder is successful, is it good?" Would he have been able to combine a coward with a criminal so masterfully? How would he have managed to let us feel that Macbeth would never have become a criminal, would never have dared such an impossible deed, had it not been for the instigation of his wife together with his own strong belief in the witches' prophecies—that is, had Macbeth not been weak-willed and superstitious? How could he otherwise have spiritualized Macbeth's crime with so much internal moral suffering and not make him detestable? Aldridge's thoughtful rendering of the role enabled him to shed light on such matters that otherwise could have faded into the background.[11]

In other words, in Macbeth Aldridge was able to illuminate and explain the most difficult aspects of this character, ground the drama psychologically, and provide it with a correct historical perspective.

It would seem a challenge for a southerner like Aldridge to play a northerner like Macbeth with a nature so remote from his own, but Aldridge was as natural and genuine in *Macbeth* as he was in *Othello*. His Macbeth was a stern northern warrior, all of whose passions appeared to be locked inside his armor. Only his insatiable thirst for power breaks through this armor and pushes Macbeth to murder the king and seize the throne. He deals the mortal blow to Duncan not as a leader to a leader, not as a rival, but as a cowardly murderer who is afraid of the rustling of his own clothes. Aldridge's Macbeth is a son of his century: he is superstitious, and he finds incentive for destroying Duncan

---

11   Bazhenov, *Sochinenia i Perevod*, 1:183.

in a witch's prophecy. In this proud and powerful man there lives a fear of his own crime. And only when ominous danger calls Macbeth to the battlefield again is the warrior in him born anew, and he refuses to retreat from his enemy. He falls slain but undefeated.

Aldridge was so consistent historically and psychologically in his representation of Macbeth that spectators were glued to the stage from the very first scene. One of them exclaimed, "What a depth, what naturalness in Aldridge's acting, in his body positioning, in his speech, in his gestures upon the very first appearance of the witches! Aldridge is able to show the way Macbeth speaks to destiny itself and feels that it is not going to be kind to him."[12]

When portraying Macbeth before the murder of Duncan, Aldridge impressed spectators with his rich and diverse mimicry. One of them recalled that

> Aldridge is superb in this scene. You see a person who is fully conscious of the baseness of his act; he is fearful, disgusted, and unwilling to do it, but something still draws him into the bedroom of the sleeping king. What is this supernatural, mysterious force that turns a kind, soft, noble person into a timid, low villain? Can it be his firm determination, his powerful will? No, this is just an insane, unfortunate passion that suddenly possesses his weak soul, and he cannot resist it. Macbeth knows very well the insanity of what he is going to do; he is aware that he will be conscience-stricken, and fear of punishment will not grant him even a moment of relief, but his mind is dimmed by passion; he already sees bloody apparitions, and the forces of darkness confuse him and possess him completely. The thought of becoming the king has crossed his mind accidentally, and his weak soul could not resist

---

12 Zvantsov, *Ira Aldridge*, 33-34.

the temptation....Macbeth's character is shown by Aldridge absolutely correctly. He is not a hero but a person who is ready to become a villain.

If we had never seen Aldridge but had only heard his yelling from behind the wings (as Macbeth is committing the murder) "Who is here?" we would have concluded that he was a great actor. Once in a lifetime one can hear this kind of cry—this is Mochalov as Karl Moor exclaiming, "Brother, brother!"

In the scene when Macbeth is asked, after the murder, if the king is awake, spectators are fearful, during the interval between the Macduff's question and Macbeth's response, that Macbeth will not find an answer and will be exposed.

Then in the scene when Macbeth pretends that he is appalled by the treacherous murder of the king, Aldridge is at the peak of artistic perfection, of refined stagecraft. He acts here a role within another role, and this is the most difficult thing in theater art. Looking at Aldridge, you know that he is pretending, but at the same time you find that he is very natural, and, had you not known the play's plot, you would not be able to notice even a trace of pretense.

In the scene when Macbeth instigates the killers, Aldridge most boldly expressed Macbeth's nature: he is ashamed and remorseful before the killers; he is looking for excuses and ingratiating himself.

The scene with Banquo's apparition is especially difficult. Here the actor must summon all the power of his imagination, all the arsenal of his psychological observations, to be able to determine how he would really talk to an apparition of the man he had killed. One cannot find a better performance of this scene.[13]

---

13 Almazov, "Aldridge on the Moscow Stage," 41:11-12.

In the feast scene "Aldridge's acting and expressiveness achieved the highest degree of perfection: his royal garment, majestic posture, with some kind of a fantastic warmth enlivening his whole personality, the graceful grandeur and meaning in each movement and word—all these features surpass anything found in ordinary theatrical performances. Nobody had every seen anything of this kind. Macbeth's speeches addressed to Banquo's ghost were filled with nobility, along with the most natural horror."[14]

From the last act one especially remembers the "mimicry of Aldridge when Macbeth runs down the hill in mute despair, and later when he fights Macduff."[15] "The battle with Macduff was at once wonderful, a truly Shakespearean, heroic ending of the tragedy, not some sort of gladiatorial contest, but a sublime portrayal of a fight in which Macbeth, falls, bleeding profusely, burdened with the wounds of a dark conscience."[16]

Aldridge became the foremost Macbeth on the Russian stage. Russian audiences owed him their first acquaintance with one of the greatest Shakespearean tragedies. The interest in Aldridge as Macbeth was so high that even in remote provinces amateur troupes were recruited in order to see Aldridge in *Macbeth*.

---

14 Zvantsov, *Ira Aldridge*, 34.
15 Almazov, "Aldridge on the Moscow Stage," 41:12.
16 Zvantsov, *Ira Aldridge*, 34.

ALDRIDGE AS OTHELLO

=============================CB=============================

One of the most famous performers of Othello, the late Vladimir V. Charsky, who had seen all the Russian and numerous foreign Othellos in his lifetime, such as Rossi, both Salvinis, Emanuel, Maggi, and Barney, told me in 1908:

> No one could play Othello like Aldridge because one had to transform into a Moor. Each of us playing Othello expends a lot of talent and energy on turning into an African and hiding a European self. This is not easy. One loses a lot of energy, and does not always succeed. You play Hamlet, Macbeth, or Lear being just yourself, without any special control over yourself, but here, as Othello, you always have to keep yourself in check: are you Moor enough as you walk on stage? Are you Moor enough when you are jealous? Aldridge did not have to do a lot: he played Othello as freely as a Spaniard would do Don Juan or a Russian would play Lyubim Tortsov. He had a Moor inside him. No one else had this freedom in playing Othello.

Vladimir N. Davydov, in his *Rasskaz o proshlom* (A Story of the Past), said, "I remember Aldridge well as Othello, although it was several decades ago. Neither Rossi, not Salvini are as memorable. His mimicry and gestures were so eloquent that one did not have to know English to understand the part."[1] The impression Aldridge produced on Russian audiences as Othello proved to be unsurpassed. In *Macbeth* Aldridge stunned with the force of his craft and created a remarkable character *despite* his physical attributes. In *Othello* he was striking in his calm wisdom that helped him invest in this character everything that he was himself: his physical self, his temperament, and his race. Judging by numerous memoirs and articles by contemporary writers, critics and artists, one can trace Aldridge's work on this character in detail, step by step.

Audiences were very excited about seeing an actor who could actually play himself in this role:

> The theater was full.... As soon as Aldridge's powerful figure appeared on stage, the theater erupted with wild applause. Aldridge bowed with dignity and began his role, emitting guttural sounds through clenched teeth. The spectators were watching him with tense curiosity, expecting something supernatural from him at any moment. But, alas, everything he did was only natural, tender, and simple. His stately figure in a red velvet Venetian costume embroidered with gold, a cloak gracefully thrown over his shoulders, his curly head, naked arms and legs covered with bracelets, the oriental armaments, and the large earrings in his ears, made him an ideal representative of the colored race. For this role he never put on any makeup and, despite his Negro face with a broad nose, fat lips, and protruding cheekbones, he appeared a handsome Venetian patrician, filled with

---

1   V.N. Davydov, *Rasskaz o proshlom* (A Story about the Past) (Moscow-Leningrad: Academia, 1930), 98.

nobility and grandeur, the chief admiral of the fleet of this proud aristocratic republic.[2]

It was the same in provincial theaters and in St. Petersburg, where he instantly triggered a comparison with V.A. Karatygin:

> There was nothing striking or showy in this figure. Othello, standing in front of the audience, had nothing in common with those we had once seen in the Alexandrinsky Theater, the Othello who was showing off and taking picturesque poses. This new Othello had simplicity, calmness, and dignity, but at first sight we could feel that behind this façade was hidden terrible force and uncurbed passions....His face was pensive and sad. When Iago made remarks about Brabantio's power and influence in the Senate, this new Othello reacted calmly and quietly:
>
>> My services which I have done the signiory
>> Shall out-tongue his complaints.[3] (Act 1, Scene 2)

Othello is the "Moor who has been touched by civilization and who remembers his royal pedigree and his military services for the Venetian republic. He is full of dignity, and with this dignity he justifies himself in front of the Senate. The Negro in him is first seen at the end of Act 2, when he stops Brabantio's servants who attack him with

---

2   V.P. Dalmatov, "Aldridge na yarmarke: rasskaz iz zapisnoi knizhki (Aldridge at the Fair. A Story from my Notebook)," *Niva* 20 (1896): 736.

3   Panaev, "Petersburg Life," 260. This essay gives the most complete and consistent outline of Aldridge as Othello. Panaev's review is all the more important as he was also a translator of *Othello* (1836) and knew Karatygin's and Mochalov's performances as Othello (at the Alexandrinsky and Maly Theater respectively).

bare swords. His earlier well-considered calmness and pomposity were taken by some spectators for coldness and an absence of liveliness in the actor."[4]

> The whole scene with the anxious Brabantio was led calmly and quietly, with the dignity and humility of a man who is convinced he is right. This was expressed through the tone of his voice when he addressed those who were prepared to protect him:

> > Hold your hands,
> > Both you of my inclining and the rest.
> > Were it my cue to fight, I should have known it
> > Without a prompter.

> And then in his addressing Brabantio:

> > Where will you that I go
> > To answer this your charge?[5] (Act 1, Scene 2)

"The regal nobility in his gait and manners, enchanting diction, perfect knowledge of the stage, *velvety* softness and flexibility in every movement, classical tranquility and fullness, but modest self-confidence"[6]—this is what Aldridge showed in the Senate scene. Othello's speech to the Senators

---

4 B. Almazov, "Aldridge on the Moscow Stage," *Russkii Vestnik* (Russian Bulletin) 40 (1862): 12.

5 Panaev, "Petersburg Life," 261. Even the paper *Nashe Vremya*, hostile to Aldridge, had to admit that his first appearance in Othello was superb: "At the very beginning of Act 1, when the Moor gives an imperious gesture to Brabantio's servants—it was one of the most successful scenes" (Anon. "Aldridge in *Othello*," *Nashe Vremya* (Our Time) 203 [September 21, 1862]: 811).

6 Zvantsov, *Ira Aldridge,* 21.

"was delivered by Aldridge with that deeply touching sincerity, by which he lives."[7]

The impressions a German spectator recorded of this speech were shared by his Russian counterpart who recalled the first scene from the first act, the one in which "the father pushes away his daughter and says, 'She has deceived her father, and may thee.'"[8] "Othello can only say, 'Come, Desdemona!' But how much boundless passion, how much childlike tenderness, is expressed in these few words! With them he is saying he will replace her father, mother, motherland, and the whole world."[9] "There was not a shade of sensuality, as in Rossi, in his acting when he came out of the Senate embracing Desdemona, or when he met her in Cyprus. He would touch her as a holy relic, love infusing his every gesture. Delight, tenderness, happiness were in his eyes and voice. Something really sincere, calm, naïve permeated all his whole being."[10]

In Act 2, Scene 3, the guardroom scene, Aldridge "impressed everyone with his grandeur. Before such an Othello all those present had to become mute and tremble. His nobility, his magnificence, his glance, sparkling as lightning, were almost impossible to bear. Everybody, innocent and guilty, at this moment turned into timid and miserable children. 'Hold, for your lives!' Only a man who has power and knows his own indestructible strength can speak these words in such a manner."[11] In this scene, when Othello stops the fight between Montano and Cassio, for the

---

7 Panaev, "Petersburg Life," 261.

8 *Leben und Künstler-Laufbahn des Negers Ira Aldridge.*

9 D. I. Sokolov, "Penza Theater," *Pezenskie Gubernskie Vedomosti* (Penza Provincial Gazette) 50 (December 9, 1864): 331.

10 Yunge, *Vospominaniya*, 171.

11 Panaev, "Petersburg Life," 261.

first time, just for one moment, Aldridge's fiery temperament breaks through. "As he observes a breach of discipline, he produces a savage sound, but the fighters instantly come to their senses, and along with them, so does their superior. As Othello reprimands his subordinates, he is still wrathful but speaks with dignity appropriate to his rank."[12] Then Aldridge shows Othello to be a person who believes in truth. He is deeply affected by this quarrel between Cassio and Montano. After the fight, which was started by Cassio, he denounces the idlers and duelists. He is ashamed of his subordinates and keeps repeating, "'Tis monstrous!" When he asks Iago what led to the conflict, Iago says with contempt, "But men are men. The best sometimes forget." Othello does not agree with this. He trusts people and believes in them, unlike the cynical Iago. Othello simply makes a gesture with his hand as if dismissing these words and thoughts. It is a very eloquent gesture, but it gave spectators an impression of how naïve he was, especially in the hands of a manipulator like Iago.[13]

Othello then says,

Cassio, I love thee
But never more be officer of mine.

Some in the audience thought there could be no other leader who would withdraw his grace and love in this quiet yet dignified way.

Act 3, in which we see constant changes in Othello's temper, feelings, and mood, revealed Aldridge's ability to disclose the complex spiritual life of his hero. "Aldridge expressed profoundly the gradual appearance and infinite changes in Othello's doomed passion. He told the story of

---

12 Almazov, "Aldridge on the Moscow Stage," 40:12.
13 Zvantsov, *Ira Aldridge*, 21.

the poor martyr unusually vividly, explaining to us in all clarity the whole process of the transformation of a small fire that only shines and gives warmth into the horrifying flame that suddenly destroyed the Moor and everything around him."[14]

As Iago is entangling Othello in a net of jealousy, he drops a phrase, "Ha! I like not that." Othello asks him, "What dost thou say?....Was that not Cassio parted from my wife?"

> These questions were spoken in a quiet, hardly audible voice, but at that moment it was necessary to watch the play of his face, in order to see how he reacted to the apparently insignificant words, "I like not that."....A shadow of suspicion fell across his spirit, and Desdemona, with her obstinate requests for Cassio must deepen that suspicion still more, but despite this, the shadow seems to disappear completely after his conversation with her, and when she leaves him, he, following her with his bright face, exclaims,
>
> > Excellent wretch! Perdition catch my soul
> > But I do love thee! And when I love thee not
> > Chaos is come again. (Act 3, Scene 3)
>
> At this moment he appears to feel an internal reproach that he allowed Iago's words to cause suspicion in his mind. Othello's internal calm is now restored: how can one suspect such a pure creature? All these emotions can be clearly read on Aldridge's face. He quietly retreats to the table and begins to examine the papers, and asks quietly, "What dost thou say, Iago?" He first calmly responds to Iago's questions about Cassio, but then he notices that Iago wants to confide something to him but does not dare to. At this point anxiety possesses him, and

---

14 Bazhenov, *Sochinenia i Perevod*, 1:180.

the words "I like not that" begin to disturb him again....Iago's cryptic remarks and responses increasingly confuse and darken his thoughts; his face with each new word of Iago becomes more and more alarmed; he begins to lose mastery over himself; his eyes begin to blaze up, and breathing heavily, he exclaims, "By heaven, I'll know thy thoughts!"

This gradual transition from confusion, from suspicion to jealousy, that increases with every word of Iago, was expressed by Aldridge with artistic subtlety and truthfulness, which revealed his deep study of the role....

One more minute and this noble Moor, trusting as a child, poisoned and wounded by his torturer, is transformed into a raging tiger, though he still battles with himself, throwing off his horrible suspicion; he still wants to doubt and tries to overcome the passion that is boiling within him. When Iago says, "I see this hath a little dashed your spirits," Othello replies, "Not a jot, not a jot." But in that answer one hears the storm that rages in his chest, and the way he pronounces these words causes a shiver to pass over the audience.[15]

Into the soul of this trustful and loving man an evil demon has begun to poor the venom of doubts! At first the Moor saw this as incredible and ludicrous, but little by little his simple soul was overtaken by discontent. 'Haply, for I am black....I am declined/Into the vale of years.' It is not only beastly jealousy that caused turmoil in his passionate soul—no!—but a feeling of injustice, regret for his lost happiness, and disappointment with his beloved as well as compassion for her: 'If she be false, heaven mocked itself. I'll not believe it.' The sense of pity toward her sneaks into his soul: is she really guilty?

But the tempter is afraid of Othello's natural kindness; he is afraid that he will forgive her and does not give him

---

15   Panaev, "Petersburg Life," 262-63.

a chance to think it over, but keeps laying it on thick with his slander, exciting Othello's worst instincts and awakening the beast in him. Yes, Othello is now a beast but one who is tortured and hunted down; in fact, when he hits Desdemona, you feel sorry for him. It cannot go on like this; his soul is strained to the extreme, so the crisis finally occurs."[16]

"She's gone, I am abused!"—this piercing cry of despair and his facial expression are impossible to describe. One can only see and hear them. A storm of applause and tears of the shaken audience ensue. The audience sees not an actor now, but a real Moor, Shakespeare's Othello, who has no other thought but that his beloved wife, whom he so passionately and tenderly loved, has cheated on him; he has no other desire than to take revenge.[17]

When Iago, having destroyed the Moor's peace with his hints, now treacherously suggests to him that he should not be jealous and offers his sympathy, then muffled sobs arise from the tormented soul of poor Othello: "O Misery! Misery! Misery!" And in those words one can hear the moans of the African actor's own tribe suppressed by slavery and also the sobs of all suffering humanity.[18]

Another spectator confirms these reactions:

In Othello's jealousy scenes Aldridge presents him not as an aggressor instilling fear but as a victim who arouses compassion and pity. The quickness, naturalness and

16 Yunge, *Vospominaniya*, 171.
17 Panaev, "Petersburg Life," 263-64.
18 Zvantsov, *Ira Aldridge*, 23.

psychological accuracy with which he transitions from one feeling to another are striking. At one moment he flies into a rage, at another he weeps and sobs like a child, and then he looks exhausted mentally and physically. His mimicry is especially striking and touching when he touches his head; this is not a routine device that many other actors use to express despair....It is not despair he wants to express here. He slowly touches his forehead and morbid convulsions pass through his face as he passes his hand over his head. One can feel passion pressuring his brain, and his mind stops functioning, exhausted under the burden of the circumstances; he is as pitiful and miserable as a helpless child."[19]

As Desdemona enters the stage to call for supper,

Othello softens up; his eyes are no longer ablaze with hatred; they begin to exude warm rays again, and his voice starts to produce soft notes again....He is quiet and humble with Desdemona, but this quietness is scary as it foreshadows a horrible storm, as the humility will turn into fury....The peace of his soul will never come back to him; this is quite clear.[20]

When Othello, tortured by jealousy, appears on the stage again with the words, "Ha! Ha! False to me?," he goes through a horrible "anguish caused by the possibility of infidelity. Sighs and complaints break out from his tormented heart."[21]

The excellent monologue—a farewell to everything dear to the Moor's militant soul—P.S. Mochalov would deliver

---

19 Almazov, "Aldridge on the Moscow Stage," 40:13.
20 Panaev, "Petersburg Life," 264.
21 Anon. "Phelka (Little Bee)," 254:1070.

with sad despair, but Aldridge with fierce despair. Yet both produced a great impression.[22]

Othello has parted with happiness and glory forever.

When the base slanders overcome Othello's reason, when his eyes can see only the hideousness of his betrayer, when his fierce passion bursts all boundaries and he throws himself at Iago in fury, the spectators shuddered in the seats.[23]

The furious Othello seizes him by the scruff of his neck, strangles him with his lion's paws, and screams:

> Villain, be sure thou prove my love a whore,
> Be sure of it. Give me the ocular proof
> Or by the worth of mine eternal soul
> Thou hadst been better have been born a dog
> Than answer my wakèd wrath! (Act 3, Scene 3)

From this moment on...throughout almost three acts, the spectators followed with sad compassion the way the great man "that loved not wisely but too well" was falling apart. Those who witnessed this performance dared not even recall all the subtle changes in the voice, gestures and mimicry with which Aldridge marked each step of his destruction, this spiritual agony.

When passion begins to rise in him, when his eyes begin burning with ominous fire, spectators can only marvel at every look, every sound coming from the depth of his shattered being:

> O blood, Iago, blood!

These words were pronounced quietly, without screaming, whereas Karatygin would scream fiercely

22 M.E. Kublitsky, "P.S. Mochalov," *Russkii Arkhiv* (Russian Archive) 12 (1875): 487.
23 Anon. "Phelka (Little Bee)," 254:1070.

when delivering this line. In Karatygin's performance, there was no transition from tenderness to violence or vice versa in the scenes with Othello and Desdemona because in Karatygin's voice there were no soft notes; in scenes of tenderness he usually dragged out the words or delivered them in singsong. But in Aldridge these transitions were marvelous. His voice was as frightening as a thunderstorm at one moment and then tender, like the quiet notes of music. From his chest sometimes screams emerged, as in the scene when he pushed Desdemona away from himself.[24]

Spectators were in mute horror observing "that scene in Act 4 when Desdemona could not return the handkerchief he had asked for. He shouts, "Devil! Devil! Devil!" How much fierce rage was spilling from poor Othello's tormented soul! Viewers did not know if they could trust what they were seeing and hearing.[25]

What was happening on stage seemed like reality—the more horrifying, the less debatable.

Having pushed Desdemona away with a wrathful arm motion— "Away!"—Othello exits the stage sobbing quietly and looking at Desdemona's face with inexpressible suffering. In no scene, in no word or movement of Act 4 did Aldridge sacrifice the truth for the sake of effect; but he did instill horror....One had only to look at him and listen to him when Iago suggests he should strangle Desdemona, and he screams, "Good, good, the justice of it pleases! Very good!"

In the final scenes of this act, his frenzy begins to subside; the frightening, destructive storm is calming

---

24 Panaev, "Petersburg Life," 270.
25 Sokolov, "Penza Theater," 332.

down. Doubts and jealousy that turned him into a beast no longer torment him."[26]

Othello becomes calmer, quieter....why would he again fly into a rage? His suspicions have been voiced; his wife's guilt has been proven; his happiness is dead irretrievably. Strong, energetic natures fly into a rage or frenzy only in the first minutes of their misfortune, while it is still fresh on their minds; the tension in their soul subsequently subsides and yields to a desire to find a way out of this depressing situation.[27]

Being sure of Desdemona's guilt has suppressed any fight in Othello. All is clear and decided for him; he is still alive and breathing but has only one wish: to take revenge. The minute he does commit this revenge, the purpose of his existence will have been achieved. After the storm that devastated everything inside him and brought about the final horrible catastrophe, life is no longer possible.[28]

There are a large number of reviews and reminiscences about Act 5. If we ignore a biased article in *Nashe Vremya* arguing that "the last scenes were the weakest of them all: we saw a man who is not smitten by grief but just tired of too much acting,"[29] we will see that all the reviews are similar. In Act 5 Aldridge reached extreme heights of acting craft and creative inspiration. In order to retain the complete character of the audience's impression in all aspects, we will cite a few statements that came from writers (I.I. Panaev, B.N. Almazov), theater critics (A.N. Bazhenov, K.I. Zvantsov), a legal scholar (A.F. Koni), an actor (V.N. Davydov), and an artist (Ye.F. Yunge).

---

26 Panaev, "Petersburg Life," 271.

27 Almazov, "Aldridge on the Moscow Stage," 40:13.

28 Panaev, "Petersburg Life," 271.

29 Anon. "Ira Aldridge in *Othello*," 811.

In one of the rooms of the Bakhrushin Museum one can see a portrait of Aldridge as Othello. He is portrayed at a moment when he enters Desdemona's bedroom and says with great sadness:

> It is the cause, it is the cause, my soul.
> Let me not name it to you, you chaste stars,
> It is the cause. (Act 5, Scene 2)

On his face one can see great sorrow and calmness. Everything has been decided. Severe cold has frozen his heart. He is now going to kill what he loves most—Desdemona—and then will kill himself. This impression is confirmed in I.I. Panaev's memoir about Othello's last scene: "When Aldridge enters the bedroom in Act 5, we no longer see the former frenzied Othello. He is calm but this is a terrible calmness. Desdemona's death is also his own death. His movements are calm, the sound of his voice is soft and tender, and his facial expression is that of firm resoluteness softened by deep sorrow."[30]

> He enters the bedroom of his sleeping wife, carefully shuts the door, and meticulously opens the curtain over her bed....But his calmness is horrifying! This is the calmness of a man with a strong soul who has firmly decided to commit a bloody crime, deeming himself entitled to it. This is the calmness of a person who is grief-stricken and fully conscious of the fact that he has forever lost his treasure.[31]

> The Moor's nobility of soul is at work here too: he enters the bedroom not like a beast but as a judge, a chastener of

---

30 Panaev, "Petersburg Life," 271.
31 Almazov, "Aldridge on the Moscow Stage," 40:13.

evil; he finds an outlet for his torments in the decision he has made. Now he is calm: she must die, but he does not want to condemn her soul nor stain her body with blood.[32]

The strongest impression of this scene was produced by V.N. Davydov:

> I will never forget the scene of Desdemona's suffocation and the following scene of Othello's spiritual awakening. I still remember his wonderful acting when he approaches Desdemona's bed, casts aside the curtain, and, with a dagger in his hand, lights her face with a lamp. One can see a feeling of tender love on his face, along with grave doubts, sad despair, hatred, and fury. The combination of all these emotions touched the audience deeply and left an indelible impression.[33]

He looks at his victim with endless love, and with a groan says, "Yet she must die, else she'll betray more men."[34]

He gives her a parting kiss, tender, chaste and horrifying, like a farewell kiss given to the dead.[35]

At this fatal moment, watching the actor impersonating Othello, you almost forget about the victim. Othello arouses more sympathy and pity from you! An odd contradiction....Oh, how this black child, transformed involuntarily into an executioner, treats his victim tenderly and softly, asking her in a harrowing voice. "Have you prayed tonight, Desdemona?" What bloody tears are heard in that voice![36]

---

32 Yunge, *Vospominaniya*, 171.
33 Davydov, *Rasskaz o proshlom*, 98.
34 Panaev, "Petersburg Life," 271.
35 Yunge, *Vospominaniya*, 171.
36 Panaev, "Petersburg Life," 271.

Yet at the same time Aldridge pronounces these words calmly and simply.[37]

So far, despite the sixty years that have elapsed, I still remember [Aldridge's Othello] as if he were alive, possessed and obsessed with the thought of revenge on his unfaithful wife. He cannot stand on his feet; he becomes weak in his knees; he heavily sits on a chair by her bedside and does not know how to reach the end of his interrogation, does not know what to do with his hands itching to strangle Desdemona; he slaps his knees with them and squeezes his thighs in agony—he is as awful and irreversible as a raging storm.[38]

In front of us there is a Moor who is focused on the necessity of an horrific revenge. And here again Aldridge's face—his fiery eyes and trembling lips—produce an indescribable effect. The scene of Desdemona's assassination inspires horror. The poor victim's explanations, instead of taming the Moor, only irritate him even more, as he is convinced of her guilt....Aldridge's acting in this scene is really tragic.[39]

Desdemona's protestations about her innocence, reminding him of Cassio and the handkerchief, infuriate Othello: he flames up for the last time, like a lamp just before it is ready to go out.[40]

---

37 Almazov, "Aldridge on the Moscow Stage," 40:13.

38 A.F. Koni, "Iz dalyokogo proshlogo" (From the Remote Past), in *Sto let Malomu teatru 1824-1924* (Maly Theater Centennial), ed. Alexandr Rafailovich Kugel (Moscow: Russkoe Teatralnoe Obshchestvo, 1924), 96.

39 R. Zotov, "Petersburg Chronicle: The African Tragedian Aldridge in Shakespeare's *Othello*," *Sankpeterburgskie Vedomosti* (St. Petersburg Official Gazette) 252 (November 16, 1858): 1478.

40 Panaev, "Petersburg Life," 272.

When Desdemona learns about Cassio's death, she shudders and begins to cry. The Moor is seized by an unlimited frenzy. He throws himself at the shameless woman who has the nerve even in her last moments to express her criminal love. He does not give her time to say her last prayers.[41]

"But while I say one prayer!" she exclaims.

But Othello, afraid the sounds of her seductive voice will soften his heart yet again, with eyes closed, so that the sight of her beautiful face will not make him pity, throws himself at her and commits the murder.[42]

As if he murdered himself, he then falls down the stairs with a loud wail.[43]

He is drained of all energy now; his hands, which had done the murder, are hanging; he is now weak and stumbling, like a child.[44]

But presently there is a knock on the door. Aldridge turns his face to the audience, and now it has changed: Othello is no longer the criminal; there is fear on his face.[45]

Emilia's knocking at the door embarrasses him....He sits down with his back to the bed; he does not dare to look around and cannot open the door for Emilia, just sits there mumbling, "My wife, my wife. What wife? I have no wife."

---

41 Almazov, "Aldridge on the Moscow Stage," 40:13.
42 Panaev, "Petersburg Life," 272.
43 Yunge, *Vospominaniya*, 172.
44 Panaev, "Petersburg Life," 272.
45 Almazov, "Aldridge on the Moscow Stage," 40:13.

The knocking intensifies. "I had forgot thee. Oh, come in, Emilia." He then closes the bed curtains to conceal the crime scene and opens the door.[46]

A.N. Bazhenov writes,

When Desdemona responds to Emelia's question ("Oh, who hath done this deed?") with her last words ("Nobody. I myself. Farewell."), and Othello is by her side, having covered his face with his hands, one cannot help wishing he would not take them off lest he show his horrible expression. One can feel that a million knives are cutting his heart with these last words in which she declares herself guilty of her own death and asks Emilia to send her regards to her husband, while he is there by the bedside, frightened of her dying voice. It is terrifying to watch this. There is as much truth in Aldridge's performance as there is in life itself.[47]

When Montano, Gratiano, and Iago enter, and when Desdemona's innocence becomes obvious to Othello, a terrible groan comes from his chest.[48]

A.F. Koni says, "I still hear him screaming '"Desdemona! Desdemona!" full of unbearable despair, without words in any human language to describe it.[49]

A. De-Ribas, a chronicler of old Odessa, shares his impressions:

Of those Odessa residents who attended the performances of the black tragedian, who cannot still hear the savage,

---

46 Panaev, "Petersburg Life," 272.

47 Bazhenov, *Sochinenia i Perevod*, 1:180.

48 Panaev, "Petersburg Life," 272.

49 Koni, "Iz dalyokogo proshlogo," 96.

beastly howl with which Aldridge shook the theater in the last act of *Othello*, when the jealous Moor learns about strangled Desdemona's innocence? This howl filled all the space in the world and the universe as a curse of the evil deed just committed. Aldridge rushed around the stage, tore his hair and clothes, as if searching for a way to annihilate himself. It was both pitiful and terrifying to hear and see him.[50]

In a feverish movement he throws himself onto Iago to tear him to pieces, but he is restrained, and he screams, "Are there not stones in heaven/But what serve for thunder?" He then gets lost in thought, strikes himself on the forehead, and declares almost in a whisper: "O fool! fool! fool![51]

In despair he calls for Desdemona, repeats her name and shakes her corpse in an effort to wake her up, resurrect her.[52]

He then covers her with kisses.[53]

Othello, having given way to repentance, rushes toward Desdemona's body and embraces her, repeating her name endlessly. There was no one in the audience who would not be crying and feeling sorry for Othello, as though he were a child lost in his own feelings.[54]

After the murder there is a drama within a drama in which Aldridge gradually realizes his own blindness and

---

50 Alexandr De-Ribas, *Staraya Odessa* (The Old Odessa) (Odessa: Kraft, 1913), 122.
51 Panaev, "Petersburg Life," 272.
52 Almazov, "Aldridge on the Moscow Stage," 40:13.
53 Panaev, "Petersburg Life," 272.
54 Davydov, *Rasskaz o proshlom*, 98.

Iago's villainy and carries this feeling of tragic pity (catharsis) to its extreme limits. Seeing off the servants who have come to remove the dying Emilia, Othello listens with rapt attention to their quiet babble, and finally gives way to complete repentance. In an ecstasy, crying and repeating her name, he throws himself at Desdemona's deathbed and embraces her for the last time. His childlike weeping, atoning for his tragic crime, shows his everlasting love.[55]

Although such a scene should have exhausted Aldridge's artistic powers, he still had enough energy in store that his suicide, with its calm and frightening simplicity, produced the strongest impression.[56]

From that moment the terrible, enraged Moor becomes more harmless than a baby. Look at the artist. You see a person drained of all power by hellish tortures and sufferings, who has reached, according to Shakespeare, the rock where his final journey ends.[57]

Othello found something to calm his soul.[58]

One cannot watch the artist's face without inner pain when he says his last words:

> Then must you speak
> Of one that loved not wisely, but too well.[59] (Act 5, Scene 2)

Suddenly Othello straightens up and transforms into the former worthy servant of Venice. His famous speech to the state's envoys he pronounces hastily, stuttering, without any effect, and at the end with one motion he slashes his

---

55 Zvantsov, *Ira Aldridge*, 25.

56 Yunge, *Vospominaniya*, 172.

57 Panaev, "Petersburg Life," 272.

58 De-Ribas, *Staraya Odessa*, 121.

59 Panaev, "Petersburg Life," 272.

own throat....The public emits a scream of horror and stands up from their chairs, but the tragedy is not over yet.[60]

Aldridge dies like no other actor could. Agonized and moaning, he rushes toward Desdemona and, as though unworthy of her, falls down dead without reaching her bed.[61]

We have had so many impressions of Aldridge as Othello! They were all shaped as one general impression[62] that almost never is the case, as usually spectators differ in their estimates of an artist, critic, writer, or an actor's performance. One has to be truly exceptional to get a unified response to his performance.

---

60 Anon. "Aldridge as Othello," *Odesskii Novosti* (Odessa News) 20 (January 27, 1866), 50. Reprinted in De-Ribas, *Staraya Odessa*, 123.

61 De-Ribas, *Staraya Odessa*, 123.

62 If we disregard the biased reviews in *Nashe Vremya* (even in those, Acts 1 and 3 of *Othello* were considered successful), we may single out only V.I. Rodislavsky, among those who wrote on Aldridge negatively. He argued that "In none of the scenes in the tragedy could we catch any moments of genuine inspiration (with the exception of the scene in Act 4, when Othello beats Desdemona); everywhere we saw the same diction, the same declamation, albeit excellently done." For Rodislavsky, Aldridge was an actor of static representation, and he contrasts him with the uncurbed inspiration of Mochalov. Rodislavsky's remarks originally appeared in a letter to the editor entitled "Aldridge and His Performances in Kazan," *Russkaya Stsena* (The Russian Stage) 4/5 (1865): 97-113, and were later quoted by M. Karneev in "Dva slova po povodu *Othello* (A Few Words Regardin *Othello* on the Stage of the Maly Theater)," *Yezhegodnik imperatorskikh teatrov* (Yearbook of the Imperial Theaters) (1907-08), 171. [Signed M. K-eev.]

This role appeared to be created specially for him, or else he for it. I doubt that any other actor could possibly portray this character with so much intensity, showing him in equal measure as impressionable, trusting, honest, gentle, and fierce.[63]

With these words Ye.F. Yunge expressed the common impression of most of Aldridge's spectators. Russian theater audiences of the 1850-60s compared Aldridge's acting in *Othello* with that of the other famous actors of the period and arrived at the same conclusion as Yunge did. Sokolov, a reviewer of Aldridge's performances in Penza, wrote,

We remember vividly such Othellos as Y.G. Bryansky, P.S. Mochalov, and V.A. Karatygin. These great artists differed from one another in style, and the impressions they left were not the same. Aldridge was beyond compare: he was fully independent, creative, and imaginative. His interpretation of Othello was not only a product of intelligence and thoughtfulness but also that of a passionate, loving, tropical nature. He did not think about passion: it poured out of his burning heart. Just as Ole Bull's fiddlestick[64] produces at one moment gentle feelings and at another fervent sentiments from the maestro's heart, Aldridge's voice rips from his bosom different feelings, ranging from heartbreaking tenderness to frenzied horror.[65]

Sokolov's comment coincides with that of I.I. Panaev, a translator of *Othello*, who had seen this tragedy performed by all the famed Russian actors mentioned by the Penza author, as well as by renowned European actors:

---

63 Yunge, *Vospominaniya*, 171.
64 Ole Bornemann Bull (1810–1880) was a Norwegian violinist and composer.
65 Sokolov, "Penza Theater," 331-33.

We saw *Othello* several times both on English and on Russian stages, in St. Petersburg and in Paris, but we never before experienced such a breath-taking, deep impression, as the one that Aldridge made on us; no one else was able to portray this Moor in such fullness and truthfulness; no one previously made it possible for us feel the grandeur of Shakespeare's creation....

In Aldridge we saw the real Othello for the first time: simple-hearted like a child and at the same time uncontrollable like a beast. We saw for the first time a complete actor, able to offer a nuanced depiction of jealousy with all its horror and ugliness, together with the most passionate love in all its attractive, tender charm. And such was the power of the actor that, upon leaving the theater after the performance, we did not have the usual feeling of heaviness and depression after this drama. The actors we had seen before as Othello understood this role mainly from an external perspective, seeing it only as an opportunity to shine, produce effects, and win applause the easy way: by frantic screams and picturesque poses. Or alternatively, someone like Macready who would be cold and fail to evoke any sympathy despite his serious study of the role. Aldridge, in contrast, brightened and animated the role of Othello by his internal flame, which gave him his power as a tragedian....After his performance one is left only with compassion for this unfortunate sufferer, and this was precisely what Shakespeare wanted his audiences to feel toward Othello.[66]

Panaev mentioned William Charles Macready, a famous English tragedian (1793-1873) who was one of the best performers of Othello. The actor Davydov, as we know already, named two others: Ernesto Rossi (1830-96) and

---

66 Panaev, "Petersburg Life," 273.

Tommaso Salvini (1828-1913), but he admitted that even their acting "could not remove Aldridge-Othello" from his mind.[67]

If we summarize all these impressions, we can see Aldridge's amazing achievement in its entirety, with his main accomplishment being a faithfulness to Shakespeare's text.

Aldridge had never read Pushkin but his performance echoes Pushkin's observation: "Othello is not jealous by nature—quite the opposite, he is trusting." This is the trustfulness of a straightforward and noble nature that never lies and never sees falsity in others; the credulity of a pure heart that has retained its childhood forever. Aldridge's Othello is not a savage: he is enlightened not less than any Venetian around him, but he has not been damaged by the lies and deception of their treachery, both political and mundane. All his faith in humanity is contained in his love for Desdemona. She is a human being in the highest and best sense, and he responds not with a dark passion, not with the tight attachment of a happy possessor of a beautiful woman, but with a deep human feeling. Therefore even the slightest betrayal of this faith is for him a catastrophe. For Othello to believe that Desdemona is guilty means that "there is no truth on earth or maybe even in the heavens" (Pushkin).

Aldridge focused special creative attention not on Othello's jealousy but on his fight with it, on his own frightening battle with himself as a human being in the depth of whose soul a previously dormant beast is awakening. Aldridge brought captivating dramatic tension into Othello's relationship with Iago, who destroyed his humanity and awoke the beast in him. At times Aldridge's acting was concentrated in his face: it reflected very

---

67 Davydov, *Rasskaz o proshlom*, 9.

realistically the torments of shame Othello felt for feeling jealous, then the fleeting joy of having achieved a temporary victory over himself, only to be followed by new despair after a new defeat. But when the beast broke loose in the scenes of Act 3, Aldridge was indeed frightening. The audience was stunned by the horror, and even some of his supporting players were terrified. The horror was caused not only by his fiery temperament or by the screams of his powerful voice but also by the profound combined expressiveness of his actions, sounds and words. His famous outburst in Act 3, "Oh, blood, blood, blood!" was spoken quietly but this confession froze everyone with its power, its perfect sincerity. In Act 5 Aldridge was quiet, thoughtful and focused: he was on his way to murder Desdemona as if to a funeral of someone dear to him who was destined to die. Desdemona's grief at the news of Cassio's alleged death would cause Othello's indescribable rage, but Aldridge played the murder scene itself without any shades of naturalism. Unlike any other Othello, he went to kill her with his eyes closed. He seemed to be hiding from himself; he was afraid that if his eyelids were to be lifted, he would see Desdemona's suffering eyes and would forgive her for everything!

Despair and an unbridled rage at himself grew in Othello as he was being persuaded of Desdemona's innocence. This emotional breakdown was so truthful in a childlike way, so profound that the spectators forgot about Desdemona's death and felt sorry for this large black child with his great heart and powerful soul who had been deceived so impudently and betrayed so brutally!

Figure 4: Oil portrait of Aldridge as Othello

Aldridge thrilled audiences, and even his critics had to agree that his acting was impeccable, deeply thoughtful, and meticulously constructed. Othello was the most striking example of that kind of reaction, as it seemed appropriate that a "Moor" playing a Moor had every right to display jealousy and ill temper naturalistically. But Aldridge did not show either. His Othello was based on a deep humanistic truthfulness: he excited spectators by stirring lively compassion in them. The Othello he created with such artistic perfection was imprinted in the memory of his contemporaries for many years.

ALDRIDGE IN A COMIC ROLE

=============Cଔୡ=============

*G*etting to know Ira Aldridge as an actor would be incomplete if we did not look at him in a comedy. In England Aldridge acted in a number of comedies. In Russia he played only one comic role—that of the mulatto Mungo in Isaac Bickerstaffe's farce *The Padlock*. Usually this short comedy would serve as an afterpiece to his great Othello on benefit performance nights. Conservative keepers of theater traditions attacked Aldridge for taking this liberty.[1] But this liberty is understandable if one reads carefully some of the reviews of Aldridge as Mungo and compares them with facts from the black tragedian's biography.

In Russian playbills the Bickerstaffe play was called *Hard to Be a Servant of Two Masters, or A Mulatto Servant: A Jocular Comic Opera in One Act and Three Scenes*. The play's plot is extremely simple. An old rich don named Diego—similar to Dr. Bartolo in *The Barber of Seville*—has a young ward Leonora, who resembles Rosina in the same Beaumarchais play. Don Diego keeps a strict eye on his ward; whenever he leaves the house, he puts the mulatto servant Mungo in

---

1   See, for instance, the indignant review in De-Ribas, *Staraya Odessa*, 123.

charge of her. Leonora has her own Almaviva, a suitor who has learnt about the absence of the old don and, having paid some gold coins to Mungo, sneaks into her room. Mungo, who has never seen this kind of money, dances and sings. *The Padlock* is an abbreviated version of *The Barber of Seville* where the part of Figaro is now played by Aldridge.

A German critic pointed out that in this brief piece Aldridge acted as "Pierrot in the splendid grotesque style of an old comedy. It is hard to describe the little songs he sang with a bottle in his hand, amusingly staggering and dancing. In their gaiety they could set even the venerable pyramids laughing."[2]

One scene was especially hilarious: "Holding a bottle of rum in one hand and a lit candle in the other, Mungo would stick the candle into his mouth instead of the bottle. After that he would spit, laugh, show his white teeth, roll his eyes, hum something, and dance."[3]

B.N. Almazov, a poet and critic, rated the artistic significance of this small comic role of the great tragedian highly: "We also saw Aldridge in the comic opera *Mulatto* and found another confirmation of the truth that not everyone has admitted—that a truly talented actor can be equally good in tragic and comic parts. Before this farce, *Othello* was on, and everyone who wept watching Aldridge as Othello now cracked up with laughter on seeing Aldridge as Mungo. How amiable he is in this role! What truthfulness, what genuine gaiety, what comedy!"[4] "In the comic part of the mulatto Mungo Aldridge gave us a typical embodiment of good-naturedness."[5]

---

2 *Leben und Künstler-Laufbahn des Negers Ira Aldridge,* 40-41.

3 De-Ribas, *Staraya Odessa,* 121.

4 Almazov, "Aldridge on the Moscow Stage," 41:14.

5 Nazarov, "Aldridge in *King Lear,*" 25.

The Padlock is the only play in which Aldridge showed a contemporary Negro to Europeans. This little play satisfied his need to be a Negro actor who was playing a simple, ordinary Negro servant, of whom there were thousands over there, in the country of slaves. It was not by accident that he linked it to *Othello,* as it seemed to him that those were the two truths: a great and a small one about a black man.

K.I. Zvantsov wrote that in *The Padlock* Aldridge "not only showed us an example of his amazing ability to play genuine comedy of the kind that we seemed to have forgotten since Luigi Lablache (1794-1858)—a buffo bass-singer who performed in St. Petersburg's Italian Opera for many years—but also acquainted us with the type of a naïve but sly Negro slave who played a role similar to that of Figaro." Among the songs sung by Aldridge there was the one favorite of American slaves—"Opossum up a Gum Tree"[6]—the same song ridiculed so much by the English actor Matthews (see Chapter 1). "The main achievement of Aldridge," another critical essay argued, "was that he for the first time introduced a type of Negro slave on our stage, and, as far as we can judge from Beecher Stowe's novels and other works by British and American authors, he did it in a convincing manner."[7]

The comic character of a Negro created by Aldridge is worth entering into the total gallery of his roles as the one in which he expressed the same irresistible truth about human beings as was winning the hearts of his audiences in his tragic roles.

---

6   Zvantsov, "Mr. Ira Aldridge's Benefit," 603.
7   R. Zotov, "Social Notes," 1859: 4.

ALDRIDGE'S ART

══════════════════ ☙ ══════════════════

*A*stage artist can celebrate a victory when his audiences forget about him and are fully carried away by the power of a character he creates. An ideal performance would be one in which the audience, while watching it, forgets the names of the actors, director, or even the author himself, and takes what happens as real life. Russian audiences perceived many Aldridge characters in this way. "This is life itself; this is Othello himself, and this is Shylock himself"—is how writers, critics, fellow actors who saw him act would describe his work. And these assertions look absolutely plausible today.

But what was behind this great acting technique? What attributes did Aldridge possess that enabled him to be a successful actor? His physical type was most fitting for the Othello role, but for an actor of lesser talent it could be an obstacle in portraying such characters as Lear, Shylock, Richard III, or Macbeth. As he was creating these characters, Aldridge not only had to suppress his fiery emotions but also had to change something that any European actor did not have to change—his race. If in his early career in North America he played Romeo and Hamlet while being black, in

Europe he could be black only as Othello and Mungo. In all the other roles he had to assume the image of a man of a different race and use heavy makeup. While playing Lear or Macbeth, he had to change the color of his face, neck, and arms by whitening them artificially. There was also the matter of accurate racial mimicry.

In the portrait painted by Taras Shevchenko's loving hand, we see a plump man with large features, very lively eyes, fat lips, and generally an appearance that fully reflected his ancestry. To transform this manly face of a mulatto into the austere royal countenance of old King Lear or the characteristic sharp features of Shylock, a great amount of hard work was required, and it is noteworthy that Aldridge sought help from others. During his tour in St. Petersburg, as a visiting celebrity, he turned to artist M.O. Mikeshin for advice on "how to correctly dress and use makeup."[1]

Aldridge was tall. This at that time was a wonderful advantage for a tragedian. V.A. Karatygin, for instance, was very proud of his height and tried to emphasize it in all the roles he played. Aldridge, conversely, subordinated his height and manly physique to the requirements of artistic truth: as Othello the military leader he seemed almost a giant, but as Shylock he lost all his height, along with manliness. Examining Aldridge's characters and their life on

---

1 According to *Neizdannye pis'ma k A.N. Ostrovskomu* (Unpublished Letters to A.N. Ostrovsky), ed. A.A. Bakhrushin and N.L. Brodsky (Moscow: Academia, 1932), 227, M.O. Mikeshin wrote to Ostrovsky, saying, "The public is jubilant whenever an actor is able to dress and use makeup correctly. I have been asked for help in this by many—not only Samoilov, Vasiliev, Setov, Gorgunov, etc. but also by such comets as Rachel and Aldridge."

stage through the prism of his contemporaries' impressions, it is not hard to see that Aldridge tirelessly sought to master the art of controlling his body. Many actors of his time possessed the skills of artistic posture and dramatic posing. One may again recall Karatygin who in Shakespeare's *Coriolanus* was said to resemble a revived ancient Greek statue. But to change one decorative pose for another does not mean that one knows how to employ rhythmic movements that express the inner life of a character. The latter task was very important for Aldridge, who consistently worked on using his body as a rhythmic and dynamic instrument appropriate for tragedy.

No one who ever wrote about Aldridge called his voice exceptional, but all agree that he could turn it into a superb instrument for producing sounds of any strength, any pitch, and containing any needed subtleties or nuances. Some Russian spectators who saw Aldridge in the 1860s found his pronunciation too melodious and his speech too elevated. Panaev, who gave the most detailed and sympathetic review of Aldridge as Othello, said of his speech at the Senate, "It seemed to us that at certain points there were odd elevations and lowerings of his voice and a stretching of words which seemed to undermine the artistic beauty of the performance."[2] But he promptly suggested that these odd features are characteristic of English pronunciation and were not a personal peculiarity of his own. Another critic describing the powerful impression from Aldridge's acting in *King Lear* wrote, "He reconciled us with the melodiousness of his pronunciation which appeared at first too fine but can be explained very simply by the presence of long and short vowels in English."[3]

---

2   Panaev, "Petersburg Life," 263.
3   Nazarov, "Aldridge in *King Lear*," 25.

Clearly, however, one cannot explain his melodious pronunciation just by the peculiarities of the language. Aldridge came to Russia at a time when V.A. Karatygin and his acting school's elevated recitations and rhythmic melodies were being replaced by another trend in stage speech that was brought about by a change in the repertoire. Karatygin's repertoire of classical and pseudo-classical tragedy, romantic drama, and melodrama, as well as the repertoires of Kukolnik and N. Polevoy, were being replaced by realistic plays of manners by Pisemsky and Ostrovsky. This sharp turn to realistic theater entailed temporary denial of any rhythmic elevation, even where it was appropriate (as, for example, in dramas written in verse). A new dogma was thus formed: classical tragedy in verse should be performed in the same way as contemporary drama written in prose. It goes without saying that for those adhering to this dogma, Aldridge may have looked like a resurrected Karatygin who used his rhythmic speech to rehabilitate the ridiculed art of declamation. A superb rebuff of such critics was issued by Almazov: "People who criticize Aldridge probably have seen a tragedy for the first time and have never heard regular tragic actors scream and growl. They should have heard Karatygin."[4] Aldridge's "melodiousness" was really a reflection of his excellent feel for the verse rhythm, whereas Russian actors of the period had only two ways of delivering verse in a tragedy: either by reciting the words bombastically or turning the verse into prose. A refined artist of the word, Aldridge achieved both musical expressiveness and meaningful effectiveness.

This peculiarity of Aldridge's speech was of decisive importance in getting the message across to a spectator who did not know the language in which the tragedian acted. In

---

4   Almazov, "Aldridge on the Moscow Stage," 40:12.

Russia, English, unlike French, was not widely known. The very "sound" of Aldridge's stage speech, regardless of its meaning, transmitted all the states of love, hate, rage, despair, suffering, etc., that corresponded to the dramatic movement of the role. Purely "vocal" aspects of the roles — for instance, Shylock's moans when he loses his daughter, or Othello's farewell weeping over Desdemona's corpse — in Aldridge were tragic monologues without words, in which the highly dramatic effect equaled the purity of musical expression. As Zvantsov recalled, "in Aldridge's very voice, in his correct charming intonation, there was sublime poetry."[5]

In addition to musical intonation, Aldridge possessed another skill by which he could speak to audiences without words. That was the language of mime. "The black tragedian vanquished his spectators. Thanks to expressive miming he was able to make them understand a foreign language."[6] This happened at the *King Lear* performance in Moscow. That was the way it always happened. "His mimicry is superb," even the Negro tragedian's adversaries admitted.[7]

Aldridge was unrecognizable in certain roles. A spectator exclaimed with delight, "He makes himself up so wonderfully that it is hard to believe that Shylock and Othello are played by the same actor!"[8] But it was not solely a matter of effective makeup but also the art of mime. Despite the inevitability of having to change the natural color of his face in any major role except Othello, Aldridge in fact did not like to use heavy makeup. He thought that the

---

5   Zvantsov, *Ira Aldridge*, 20.
6   Nazarov, "Aldridge in *King Lear*," 24.
7   Anon. "Aldridge in *Othello*," 811.
8   V.M., "Feuilleton," *Spravochnyi listok g[ubernii] Saratova* (Directory [of the Province] of Saratov) 128 (June 18, 1864): 2.

face was a splendid instrument that the actor should strive to master to perfection. Aldridge's mimicry was not simply a sum of tricks he learned to use with his face—not just an imitation of muscle movements corresponding to this or that emotion. On the contrary, it was a direct reflection of these emotions, Panaev noted, "It is remarkable that Aldridge's face instantly reflects the slightest emotions and movements of the soul—and not the way other actors, even good ones, do, who have learned techniques for expressing sadness, joy, surprise, doubt, etc.—no! His face is a correct and deep reflection of his inner state at any given minute. It is not enough to see and hear Aldridge from afar; one has to follow the amazing acting of his face."[9]

Aldridge's gestures and movements fully corresponded to his mimicry; being simple, they were characteristic of a given personage, merging with his overall appearance and based on his character. Aldridge never skimped on movements and gestures and never used them excessively: he limited himself only to the essential. But, having become supremely simple, they acquired an especially lucid expressiveness. If Aldridge had been mute, he still would have been able to create the images of Lear and Othello that would be clear to the spectator.

In the history of theater one can hardly find another example of the power of mime and gesture akin to the famous finale of Aldridge's Shylock. Without using any words or sounds, Aldridge was able to portray Shylock's indignation, his hatred of infidels, as well as his fear and defenselessness, blending these emotions together into synthesis of tragic despair. Sokolov said, "Aldridge's voice is perfection itself, and he uses it like a musical instrument; his mimicry is outstanding; his firm skin and flexible facial

---

9   Panaev, "Petersburg Life," 262.

features produce wonders. When, in emotional scenes, these tools are used together, Aldridge seems an unearthly, supernatural creature. The flow of his passions and the music of his voice are truly amazing."[10] The testimony of this Penza critic is confirmed by another in Tambov: "One can only be amazed and not believe one's eyes, seeing it was possible for Aldridge, reciting in a foreign language and using mime and gestures, to so lucidly and correctly express human passions."[11]

Aldridge prepared a role and played it as though he knew Coquelin's aphorism that in an actor there coexist materials and a sculptor, that an actor's creative work is essentially the work of a sculptor on materials contained within himself. V.N. Davydov, who as a young actor took part in one of Aldridge's performances, recalled,

> I was really struck by Aldridge's extraordinary ability to take up any part in a role, any tumultuous scene, right off the bat. I remember once, during a rehearsal of an emotional scene, a loud noise erupted backstage. Aldridge, who was then weeping with what seemed to be such deep sincerity, suddenly stopped the scene and quietly asked that the noise behind the curtain be stopped, and then, after it had ceased, he carried on with his sobbing in a manner that was no different than what it had been earlier. Like a violinist of genius, he could take on any difficult passage at any time.[12]

---

10 Sokolov, "Penza Theater," 333.

11 Anon., "Aldridge in Tambov: Local News," *Tambovskie Gubernskie Vedomosti* (Tambov Provincial Gazette) 43 (October 1864), 341.

12 Davydov, *Rasskaz o proshlom*, 101.

It appeared to his audiences that Aldridge on stage was fully possessed by his role: he seemed like a swimmer who makes all the right movements with his legs and arms but in reality has just succumbed to the rage of the surf that is carrying him. This impression was shared by most Russian actors who played with him. Actress M.I. Velazarii tells us a story she heard from her grandmother, actress A.P. Novistkaya-Kapustina (1818-1908), who played with Aldridge in Kharkov and Kiev:

> Aldridge had a fiery temperament. In Act 5 of *Othello* he strangles Desdemona. Aldridge's eyes would become bloodshot and foam was coming from his mouth. Grandma was scared to death. Her lines slipped her memory, and she stopped for a moment—the scene was going on at an insane pace.
>
> Suddenly she heard Aldridge's whisper in her ear:
> "Nishevo, nishevo." (It's all right, it's all right.)
>
> And then in English again—a scream of fury. His hands were at her throat. He was suffocating her with a pillow. The same scary face, and then another quick whisper:
>
> "Nishevo, ne boysia." (It's all right, don't be afraid.)
> Neither the public nor even the actors who were standing backstage noticed anything. At the end of the act—a storm of applause. And poor Desdemona came forward, trembling from the horror she had experienced, hand in hand with the black monster who was smiling at her calmly.[13]

Both these cases serve as classic examples of an artist's creative self-control. V.P. Dalmatov offered an additional illustration from Aldridge's performance in Rybinsk:

---

13 M.I. Velizarii, *Put Provintsialnoi aktrisy* (A Provincial Actress's Path) (Leningrad and Moscow: Iskusstvo, 1938), 14-15.

When in the last act Desdemona lay down on the bed with her legs where her head should have been, it caused some confusion, since pedantically strict Aldridge never altered the *mise en scène* and flew into a rage at any deviation. In this case, instead of giving his monologue looking at Desdemona with the curtain open, he shut it closed, seized the scared-to-death Desdemona as though she were a feather, tenderly pressed her against his fat lips, whispered something softly in her ear, and placed her in the appropriate position. Then he opened the curtains again and somberly continued his monologue.[14]

However high Aldridge's rage would elevate him, however obsessed with the emotional side of a role he was, he never and under no circumstance lost the essence of a character he had created. Actress A.N. Mochalova, known under the stage name Danilova, also played Desdemona with Aldridge. She recalls,

He had everything calculated, each utterance, and each step. It took forty times for him to rehearse one scene....If he was accustomed to playing a scene on this rug, for instance, he would never step over to a different one... And then he would make you do this scene only the way he wanted you to, before he was satisfied. If there was a stain on the floor and he was used to falling down on this spot, you can be sure that no matter what agitation he would be in, he would fall down on this very stain.[15]

In the period when Aldridge toured Russia and Europe, there was no theater director in today's sense, someone who has created the performance and is responsible for its creative unity. From the stories just cited, it is clear that

---

14 Dalmatov, "Aldridge na yarmarke," 736.
15 Anastasia Alekseevna Verbitskaya, *Moemy chitateliu* (To My Reader) (Moscow: I.N. Kushnerev, 1908), 14.

Aldridge was not only a performer but also a director: he demanded from his partners that they be subordinate to his creative design, and he himself never ruined it with outbursts of improvisation. One needs to add that there were two Aldridges. One was akin to an exemplary opera singer who performed his part with absolute musical precision. The other, unseen to anyone, conducted his part in strict accordance with the author's score. Russian actors who left memoirs about acting with Aldridge are inclined to see this "calculation by a serpentine wisdom" as central to his art, this triumph of exceptional technique that allowed him to imitate passion or reproduce any feeling at will at any time. This conclusion was deeply erroneous. Aldridge was indeed perfect at what is sometimes simply called an "actor's technique." He was especially interesting to most Russian actors of his time, for whom the old technique of Karatygin had been lost and a new one, that of deep realism, had not yet been found. But for Aldridge mastering a technique meant not limiting the actor's art but always matching his creative "I want" with a methodical "I can."

At the height of his powers Aldridge could always *implement* masterfully anything that he had *conceived* as a profound artist. The art of *conception* in Aldridge was as deep as his craft of *execution*. Trying to understand the creative character of the Negro tragedian, critics compared him with almost all the other prominent contemporary actors, finding both similarities and differences. Poet and critic Théophile Gautier, upon seeing Aldridge in St. Petersburg, expressed his amazement: "We had been anticipating a vigorous style, somewhat uncontrolledly energetic, a little wild and fierce, after the manner of Kean; but the Negro tragedian, doubtless in order to appear no less cultured than the white man, acts wisely and restrainedly, in a majestic style resembling that of Macready....In any event, he produced an enormous impression."[16] Panaev, as we know, on the contrary, denied any resemblance between Aldridge and Macready. Almazov insisted on Aldridge's affinity with Mochalov, while others denied it. The contradictions in these opinions confirm Aldridge's independence as a creative personality.

But, while insisting on Aldridge's kinship with this or that contemporary, no one ever argued that there was any resemblance between his Othello, Lear, Macbeth, or Shylock with any character created by any of those actors. Quite the contrary, Aldridge impressed by the originality of his conceptions, by his unexpected bravery in interpreting Shakespeare's characters who before Aldridge had been known in more than a hundred critical interpretations and stage versions. Even Aldridge's enemies who attacked him for, say, portraying Shylock not as a petty, stingy villain but as a man of great feelings and strong character, could not deny the originality and independence of his construction of Shakespearean characters.

Only a very imperfect view of Aldridge's characters is accessible to us, available through the eyes of his spectators, but even this faulty glimpse allows us to see that any character—be it fiery Othello or reserved Macbeth—grew out of Aldridge's deep thinking and extraordinarily accurate observation of human nature. A character's inner world, his social and cultural position in life, his appearance, face, gait, everyday habits, national formation—all these aspects were studied by Aldridge until they became absolutely clear to him. When Aldridge would completely master the inner

---

16 Pierre Larousse. *Grand Dictionnaire Universel du XIXe Siècle* (Paris: Administration du Dictionnaire, 1866-1890), Vol. 26, supplement, 86.

content of a character and all the peculiarities of his being and behavior, he would look for the simplest but also the most expressive means of rendering this character to the public. But it would be wrong to think that the whole creative process for Aldridge boiled down to grasping the "essence" of a character and carefully studying the historical and everyday existence of such a person and then straightforwardly portraying it on stage. This evaluation of his creative activity oversimplifies it; an intelligent and educated individual, he would first clarify for himself the way this or that character needed to be played and then, from his vast arsenal of stage techniques, he would find methods and devices with which he could most effectively convey that concept into a stage figure.

This was not the way V.V. Samoilov, Aldridge's antagonist, operated. All his artistic attention was geared toward searching for the most *characteristic* traits in a human being—be it Inspector Rostakovsky or King Lear—and diligently assembling a collection of these *characteristic* traits, displaying them primarily in his appearance, the way he looked. Samoilov tried to build tragic *characters*. Unsurprisingly, his King Lear was a decrepit, sick old man; aside from his age, any of the formidable poetry and human truth of the Shakespearean character would disappear. Samoilov was a typically great actor of *representation*.

Aldridge, by contrast, with all his mastery of makeup, gesture, movement, and declamation, was much more capable of *representation* than Samoilov. But it would be a mistake to think that Aldridge was only a master of representation and was incapable of emotional experience. Quite the opposite, he was fully focused on disclosing the inner world of his characters. In this regard, one of the most valuable accounts is that of critic and poet B.N. Almazov, who was close to A.N. Ostrovsky and P.M. Sadovsky. With the Moscow tours of Eliza Rachel (1853) and Adelaide Ristori in mind, he wrote,

> Aldridge has nothing in common with those Western stage celebrities who have recently visited us. His strengths are not in artificial poses and gestures, not in melodiousness of diction, not in the well-studied solemnity of a tragic gait. No, he is less concerned about these superficial aspects of acting and concentrates attention only on the inner meaning of what he says. He too is concerned with gait but he walks naturally, like a human being, not like a tragedian. He is not concerned with achieving ballet-like movement on stage but rather with developing a high, truthful understanding of art, based on a deep knowledge of the human soul and an ability to feel the subtle movements of that soul noticed by Shakespeare — this is the essence and strength of his acting.

Clarifying Aldridge's status as an actor of internal truth rather than external credibility, Almazov went on to say,

> One can call Aldridge a psychological actor. Psychological truth is the main target of his acting. He tries to be as natural as possible in portraying subtle movements of the soul in a character he plays. His acting therefore is very serious, and only connoisseurs of art and of Shakespeare's plays can pass judgment about it.[17]

Exactly the same idea is found in an article by N.S. Nazarov:

> I am sure that all of us who saw Aldridge in all his roles had a chance to notice that he is not after external effects but rather internal aspects of acting; the expression of subtle psychic emotions prevails over expressing a strong passion. In Othello the growling of an African lion was

---

17 Almazov, "Aldridge on the Moscow Stage," 40:12.

heard much more rarely, if at all, than the moaning of a sick soul; the murder of Desdemona did not make as strong an impression on the public as Othello's despair when he learns the truth and wants to resurrect his beloved wife.[18]

A "calm" Aldridge, an artist of focused feeling, reserved passion, internal suffering shook the public no less and even more than an exponent of boiling fury, flaming passion and tragic frenzy. It was enough to recall "calm" and "mute" scenes in *Othello, Lear,* and *Merchant of Venice* when all the public's attention was taken up by the truth of the internal struggle and hidden feelings, enough to recall that even the famous phrase by Othello: "Oh, blood, blood, blood!" that would be pronounced by most tragedians with frenzied passion, was delivered by Aldridge quietly, almost in a whisper. Depicting Macbeth's step toward murder, a German critic was stunned by Aldridge's calmness in playing him:

> This quiet scene was certainly not as dramatic as when a Macbeth storms in, crying out. But what deep natural truth lay in this vacillation and anxiety between decision and deed! It was as if the colored hero, with a look and gesture, had transformed Hamlet's famous statement *To be or not to be* into *To kill or not to kill.*[19]

This critic emphasizes the fact that Aldridge preferred psychological truth, in all its richness of nuances, to external aspects of tragedy that would be so easy to show, relying on one's "art of representation."

One provincial Russian reviewer, delighted by Aldridge in *Othello,* saw his main strength as the ability to keep silent

---

18 Nazarov, "Aldridge in *King Lear,*" 25.
19 *Leben und Künstler-Laufbahn des Negers Ira Aldridge,* 34.

and establish silence on the stage, providing a "broad range of effects, from deathly silence to some of the most furious sounds."[20] Aldridge captured the attention not only of provincial audiences and critics but also of commentators such as Panaev who were familiar with European theater, and those like Almazov, who admired Mochalov, not by *showing* Shylock's emotions or Othello's passions but by allowing spectators to *experience* them. For the majority of Aldridge's spectators, he remained an actor of genuine spontaneity, powerful outbursts, and passionate shocks. He really did exhibit all these diverse traits.

Aldridge was once asked how he could fall down stairs after the suicide in *Othello,* and what measures did he take not to get hurt? He laughed in his usual good-natured way and replied, "What can I do? I am all covered by bumps and bruises. Do you think I remember anything in that moment? Do you think I know where I am falling? God must be protecting me somehow."[21]

Aldridge had the exceptional ability of captivating the public: a spectator was always a prisoner of those powerful feelings and passions that the actor lived through as Othello, Lear, etc. But this was because the actor himself was a prisoner of the same feelings while living the life of the character on stage. Aldridge had another rare quality: he could play a role for the hundredth time with the same sincerity and freshness as he did the first time. The public felt that regardless of how many times they might see Othello, every time the actor had the Venetian Moor living inside him who would then burn to ashes in the flames of unprecedented sufferings. The word "emotion" was not included in the lexicon of theatergoers back in the 1850s and

---

20 Anon. "Aldridge as Othello," 50.
21 Yunge, *Vospominaniya,* 173.

60s, but only this term can adequately capture Aldridge's capacity to captivate the public by the sheer power and tension of his acting.

It was no accident that those who experienced the joy of this kind of capture recalled Mochalov, the greatest Russian "actor of emotion." Almazov, a fervent admirer of this "insane friend of Shakespeare's," said, "We very well remember Mochalov, who shocked and stunned us with his acting as Hamlet, Othello, and Franz Moor, and we cannot help but mention him as we speak about Aldridge. Before we saw Aldridge, we had not thought he could be similar to the Moscow tragedian, as we did not trust foreign celebrities touring Russia. But when we saw him, we noted instantly his striking resemblance to Mochalov: the same simplicity, absence of external effects, and avoidance of pseudo-classical school devices." Aldridge and Mochalov were not opposed only to the tragedians of the Karatygin school with its "measured declamation and icy words" (Lermontov) but also to such celebrated visiting tragedians as Ristori and Rachel, who were mentioned earlier. Both Aldridge and Mochalov were able to portray what is most difficult in the art of tragedy: the height and authenticity of tragic emotions coupled with the genuine simplicity of their expression. In this regard, Almazov placed Mochalov higher than Aldridge: the former "had one inimitable trait that brought him success: an outburst of the most genuine, non-artistic feeling." This "non-artistic feeling" in Mochalov broke through in his interpretations of Hamlet and Othello; as Apollon Grigoriev argued, it was this "internal spiritual tragic element" that characterized Mochalov as a person; it was this "fiery breathing" that surrounded him all his life.[22]

---

22 Apollon Grigoriev, *Vospominaniya* (Memoirs) (Moscow and Leningrad: Academia, 1930), 248-49.

Having noted this remark, Almazov went further:

> But as a conscious artist Aldridge is superior to Mochalov. Mochalov, as Belinsky accurately suggested, was not an actor but a frenzied Pythoness on her tripod....Mochalov's vivacity, albeit so genuine and authentic, quite often did not fit the person he portrayed....
>
> Aldridge was not like that. He never has these natural outbursts or inspired moments that happen to an actor without his awareness of them. He is a consciously creative artist who has everything calculated, thought over, and subordinated to the main concept of the character he plays. We do not want to claim that Aldridge is devoid of inspiration. Quite the opposite. If there is creativity, there should be inspiration as well. Yes, Aldridge surely created his roles under the guidance of high inspiration. But this inspiration always came to him in the silence of his study, where he would delve deep into the work of Shakespeare. Maybe at those moments, like Mochalov, he would alternate between pathos and icy coolness. But that was only the way he behaved in the laboratory of his creative work, where no one could see him. Mochalov's instinctive acting is like a rough draft of a great manuscript that has not yet been edited by the author, and reads like it was released before its time. Aldridge's acting is like a thoroughly corrected, well-considered work of art.[23]

One conclusion to be drawn after all these comparisons of Aldridge and Mochalov can be found in an article about Aldridge's King Lear: "He is a genuinely Shakespearean actor, just like Mochalov, but in addition to the extraordinary talent of the Russian tragedian, he also is

---

23 Almazov, "Aldridge on the Moscow Stage," 40:12.

extremely artful."[24] We could further reinforce this conclusion by quoting A.I. Herzen on Mochalov: "Mochalov was a man of outbursts that were not controlled but caused by inspiration. He was not in control of his tools—rather, they controlled him." One can argue something similar about Aldridge, but also the opposite: he was a man of outbursts and inspiration but always in submission to the tools of his great and stubborn craft. Aldridge's "devices" were always "obedient" to him. His art of representation was controlled, to use Herzen's words, by his "inspiration."

Herzen went on to say that Mochalov "knew that sometimes he was visited by a specter that turned him into Hamlet, Lear, or Karl Moor and waited for it…but the specter would not come, and what we saw instead was an actor who did not know his part well."[25] Aldridge, conversely, never waited for these visits; he himself initiated meetings with Lear or Othello, and having met with them, transformed himself into the old king or Venetian Moor wholeheartedly, just like Mochalov. Maybe Mochalov had more creative energy than Aldridge, but he did not possess the ability to transform this energy into a light that would shine on everyone at will. Aldridge did possess this power, to the utmost degree.

Russian actors oftentimes were faced with a choice between creatively *experiencing* an emotion or merely *representing* it on stage. Representing it meant being a Karatygin with his artful "artificialness" in each role. Experiencing it implied being a Mochalov with his unbridled outbursts. Aldridge destroyed this division of approaches. He did both simultaneously: he could never

---

24 Nazarov, "Aldridge in *King Lear*," 25.

25 Alexandr Ivanovic Herzen, *Byloe i Dumy* (My Past and Thoughts) (Moscow: Academia 1932), 3:78.

represent without *experiencing*. Aldridge achieved a creative union by faithfully representing what he was experiencing. This was the foundation for all his characters, from King Lear to the Negro servant Mungo. Aldridge personified a wonderful synthesis of these normally mutually inimical theatrical traditions. He was a Mochalov, but one who subordinated creative outbursts and emotional displays to the wisdom of deep art.

Zvantsov found this "complete *smoothness*," a crucial quality in all arts, at a high level in Aldridge's acting."[26] Another critic, summarizing the outcome of Aldridge's Moscow tour in 1862, wrote, "Almost all agree that this tragedian's performances are distinguished by an impeccable refinement of form, a deep thoughtfulness of stage positions, meticulous study of the represented personality, clever arrangement of the role, and striking truthfulness."[27] This wealth of artistic elements in Aldridge's acting, so striking for his spectators, was ultimately reflective of the *completeness of life*, a triumph of genuine *truth* disclosed by an artist about humanity.

To achieve this truth, Aldridge was ready to boldly break away from the shackles of conventional theater that had handcuffed other tragedians. He sought for a real life justification of every dramatic movement prescribed by a role, and persistently sought for freedom on stage. Monologues of the protagonist had to be delivered from the proscenium, according to the canons of French tragedy. This rule outlived the Sumarokov epoch in Russian theater and was observed by the tragedians of 1840s and 50s in the same manner as it had been by I.A. Dmitrievsky in the second half

---

26 Zvantsov, *Ira Aldridge*, 22.

27 N. Panovsky, "What is Going on in Moscow," *Russkii Vestnik* (Russian Bulletin) 38 (September 1862): 30-31.

of the 18th century. Aldridge broke up all these rules by creating his *mise-en-scènes* only upon the logic of internal efficiency, without obeying any canon created in the past. Zvantsov testified that "Contrary to common prejudices, he sometimes waves his palms, lifts his arms over his head, stands with his back to the public and not just in profile, often whispers or speaks in a low voice, breaks up entire monologues into small parts, many of which are delivered from the depths of the stage. In a word, he does not obey any stage convention that could harm dramatic truth."[28]

The completeness of this "dramatic truth" in some of his roles was achieved by Aldridge with varying amounts of success but his aspiration for it was always present. "The Shylock part was so saturated with inner vigor and truth that one was never reminded of the performer's personality," Bazhenov writes. He repeated the same about *Othello*: "This performance has as much truth in it as there is in real life."[29] And Yunge said in her memoir that "Aldridge's realistic style made a strong impression on me. After his first performance I wrote in my diary, 'When he enters the stage, his simplicity seems almost disagreeable.' Gradually I learned to appreciate it and became an admirer of his acting."[30]

Aldridge's simplicity of *presentation* was based on his deep comprehension of the character he portrayed which enabled him to enter the thoughts and feelings of that character. To *simply* recount or *simply* present some experience in life can only be achieved by someone who has fully known it, lived it, and mastered it. That was the case with Aldridge. The simplicity he sought had nothing to do

---

28 Zvantsov, *Ira Aldridge*, 21.

29 Bazhenov, *Sochinenia i Perevod*, 1:180.

30 Yunge, *Vospominaniya*, 172-73.

with simplifying Shakespeare's characters. Bold and consistent as a realist, he never merely reproduced the petty facts of everyday existence. Aldridge in every role tried to create a character fully warmed by the breath of life. This is why his Othello and Shylock, retaining their Shakespearean human traits, were able to stir a lively response in audiences who associated them with whole nations seeking for emancipation and freedom.

Shakespeare was for him not only the most truthful portrayer of life but also the greatest poet. This is why his Othello or King Lear were not only deeply realistic but also beautiful, highly poetic characters. Aldridge *lived* on stage; he did not just represent life. For each role he would seek to find such perfect means of expression that the character would become a marvelous work of art.

ALDRIDGE IN MOSCOW

== == == == == == == == == == == ==C8== == == == == == == == == == == ==

After his St. Petersburg tour (1858-59) the great tragedian was longing to perform for the Russian public. In the last eight years of his life only two were spent outside of Russia (1860 and 1863). Aldridge arrived in Moscow in 1862. Between September 13 and October 19 he gave fourteen performances of Shakespearean tragedies, including *Macbeth*, which was reluctantly permitted by the censors. The audience's interest in Aldridge and his success there were so large that most of his performances took place not in the Maly Theater but in the Bolshoi. Despite a slow fall season, the huge theater was packed.

The first performance, *Othello*, received the following notice in a Moscow magazine:

> The house was full…. It can be said with absolute certainty that Shakespeare could not have wished for a better performer of his great work. Othello, innocent, drawn to everything good like a child, gentle and kind like a young girl, and Othello furious, raging like a beast, lived before us on the stage. The public's delight was great, and there was no end to the applause and encores. All the praise we had read about Aldridge is no exaggeration; he is a truly enormous talent, and everyone who wants to see

Shakespeare's characters on stage must see Aldridge's performances. He will explain to you all the greatness of the extraordinary poet's works.[1]

The top theater critics devoted favorable, in-depth articles to Aldridge as an interpreter of Shakespeare. The black tragedian won over the great Shchepkin and Prov Sadovsky, the pride and joy of the Russian theater. Two testimonies need to be cited here as evidence of the younger generation's interest in Aldridge. Writer I.N. Zakharyin (Yakunin) recalled that "His acting made so strong an impression that I was under the spell of this tragedian's charm for several days....The scene in which Othello realizes Iago's treachery and Desdemona's innocence, and the way he suffers his belated remorse for the murder, brought tears to the eyes of not only the women in the audience." Stunned by Aldridge's acting, Zakharyin tried to meet him. He finally managed to see him at an English church. "I had a chance to examine his face up close," he recalled. "I was struck especially by his eyes—black, big, radiant....Many years later I saw the equally famous Salvini in *Othello* and later in *Hamlet*, but his acting did not produce the same impression on me as I had experienced in 1863 in Moscow."[2]

Aldridge's acting was that of a genius, and it roused deep interest in Shakespeare among spectators. In his memoir academician I.I. Yanzhul recounts that

My childhood imagination was strongly affected by Shakespearean plays as presented by the touring

---

1   Katin, "Notes on Moscow Life," *Razvlechenie* (Entertainment) 39 (September 20, 1862): 156-57.

2   I.N. Zakharyin, *Meetings and Memoirs* (St. Petersburg: M.V. Pirozkova, 1903), 317.

American Negro actor Ira Aldridge, who performed the major plays in many Russian cities, not just the capitals but also Ryazan, where I was a high school student. Attending the performances in Moscow during vacations and enchanted by his acting, I was deeply upset that I could not understand anything. Having learned that he would perform in Ryazan in three or four months, I decided to make an effort to learn just enough English so I could understand most of his speeches with the help of a book in my lap. With hard work and dedication I managed to achieve that goal, and three months later, with a miniature volume of Shakespeare in hand I could understand almost everything he was saying.[3]

Yanzhul's story gives us a better idea about Aldridge's actual success and its cultural significance. A.N. Bazhenov, a great connoisseur of Shakespearean theater who was not known for being generous with his praise, also wrote, "These performances were definitely the best I have ever seen in the theater: this was truly a feat of representing Shakespeare artistically."[4]

During Aldridge's second visit to Russia in 1862, a reactionary part of the public, including actors and critics, became quite disdainful of him. The papers printed more negative reviews about him than in 1858. It seemed as though he had arrived there at a good moment: serfdom was abolished and reforms were expected. But in reality calls to go back to the earlier regime were heard more often and stronger than before. Even within the Maly Theater troupe there was a negative attitude toward the black actor.

---

3   I.I. Yanzhul, *Memories of Things Seen and Experienced in 1864-1909* (St. Petersburg: Electro-tipografiya N.I. Stoikovoi, 1910), 52.

4   Bazhenov, *Sochinenia i Perevod*, 1:179-80.

Bazhenov, an expert on this subject, wrote about this with full clarity: "Aldridge was playing here under very unfavorable conditions. All the four tragedies were cut horribly; almost all our best actors (shame on them for this sin!) refused to take part in Aldridge's performances, and because of that, the roles were given out to whoever was available."[5] Rumors spread among the actors, and especially the actresses, that it was dangerous for them to perform with him because of the unpredictable nature of his savage ways.

Even during Aldridge's first tour in Russia, a popular magazine had carried a cartoon emphasizing his "lack of restraint," publishing it under the title, *Iago's Unfavorable Position When Othello Shakes him by the Collar a Bit.* Yet more expressive was another cartoon called *The Trial.* Desdemona and Othello are in front of the judge:

> *Desdemona.* Save me! This savage is going to strangle me at some point for real!
>
> *Judge.* Be careful, Mr. Othello. If you really strangle her, what will happen then?
>
> *Othello.* Not much. You will give me another Desdemona, better than this one.[6]

---

5   Ibid., 1:185.
6   Anon. "[Caricatures], "*Syn Otechestva* (Son of the Fatherland) 49 (December 7, 1858): 1487.

Figure 5: Caricature of Aldridge as Othello in Syn Otechestva,
December 7, 1858

Figure 6: Caricature of Aldridge as Othello in Syn Otechestva, *December 7, 1858*

A.A. Stakhovich, a well-known nobleman and theatergoer, once got to talk to Aldridge in Voronezh and asked how things went with Othello at the Maly Theater, where the tragedian's costar was a well-known actress, L.P. Nikulina-Kositskaya (1829-1868). Aldridge replied that the

Moscow Desdemona "was embarrassed by the rumor that he had strangled several Desdemonas in the heat of the performance and was afraid to play alongside him. This is an exaggeration," the tragedian went on, "In all my life I have played this role more than three hundred times and have strangled only two, maybe three Desdemonas and also stabbed one. I think you will agree that the percentage is very low, so she had nothing to worry about." This was so shocking to Stakhovich that he never further "interrogated the fiery tragedian."[7]

The nobleman did not catch the bitter irony of Aldridge's words. The absurd and offensive rumor about him strangling almost all his Desdemonas was started in America by his enemies and then followed him through Europe and made its way to Russia. American and English actors who despised him hoped this rumor would scare white actresses from performing with him. Knowing that this bizarre allegation continued to dog him, Aldridge teased Stakhovich with his frightening confession.

Rumors about the physical hazards of playing Desdemona opposite Aldridge's Othello remained so persistent that everyone seemed to believe them. Before Aldridge's trip to Saratov a local newspaper wrote, "Long before the performance everyone wondered who was going to play Desdemona—Ms. Medvedeva or Ms. Roslavskaya. Some argued for the former, counting on her sturdy build and strong bones to withstand the onslaught from Othello while he was strangling her; others wanted Roslavskaya, noting her superior talent."[8]

---

7 A.A. Stakhovich, *Klochki vospominaniy* (Scraps of Memories) (Moscow: N. Kushnerev, 1904), 99-100.

8 V.M., "Feuilleton," 2.

V.N. Davydov, who saw Othello in Tambov and participated in the *Othello* performance, recounts that

> Desdemona was played by a local actress, who lacked talent. In the scene when there is an erupting volcano of jealousy in Othello's chest, she must have also wanted to act and began smoothing out wrinkles on her dress with incredible calmness and indifference. Aldridge was insulted by her attitude, and running up to her, intentionally seized her arm so harshly that deep suffering and physical pain were instantly reflected on her face. Having cut his speech short, the tragedian looked at her with a smile and tenderly said, "Very good! Very thank you!"—and afterwards continued the interrupted scene. All the Desdemonas were scared of him, fearing he could really strangle them in his rage in the last scene. But every time Aldridge, in between the loud noises, with the softest voice would whisper into the ear of the actress playing Desdemona, "Don't be afraid, child," even though at times this child was around fifty years old.[9]

Davydov's story is very similar to accounts given by actress Novtskaya-Kapustina and actor V.P. Dalmatov. The rumors based on lies about Aldridge's dangerous fiery deeds were attempts to hamper his success. Aldridge, a genuine artist with new creative methods, caused irritation among adherents of the more traditional schools of thought. And the fact that this innovative artist was a Negro, not a member of a privileged race, turned this irritation into hatred.

Critic A. Ivanov, a penname for A.I. Urusov, a leftist lawyer who was later exiled from Moscow for interactions with the Nechaev group, wrote in his 1862 "Chronicle of the Maly Theater,"

---

9 Davydov, *Rasskaz o proshlom*, 104.

A certain part of the public received Aldridge coldly and with ill will. No wonder! Imagine that suddenly a man turns up out of nowhere, with his "raw flesh," to use Ms. Kokhanovskaya "apt" phrase, and puts many respectable people in danger of looking quite bad. Here, at this very Maly Theater, shortcomings of certain actors may now be exposed as Aldridge, an interpreter of Shakespeare, takes the stage, preceded by his huge reputation. How can he be judged? Or maybe we should just keep silent? The authority of many local dignitaries will be threatened. The best way out was to criticize, so they began to criticize him. Some reproached him for being too natural, others for being too artificial. And the largest number of critics— for both. These accusations were mutually exclusive and clearly did not make much sense."[10]

Some reactionary members of the audience and the press accused Aldridge of extreme naturalism and of savage-like distortion of the greatest European playwright. These were Russian variations of the American tune, "a black slave cannot play a white hero."

A conservative periodical, *Nashe Vremya*, attacked Aldridge for being a defender of Shylock in *Merchant of Venice*, not an accuser. The newspaper's critic wrote, "It turned out that Aldridge was not thinking that he was Shylock, that for the length of a few hours he had to impersonate this hater of Christians, this miser, this kike, contaminated with all the wisdom and superstitions of his tribe. No, Aldridge took Shylock aside and bossed him around as if he owned him."[11] "Bossed him around" meant that Aldridge did not play Shylock in the way prescribed by the conservative Moscow newspaper.

---

10 A.I. Urusov, *Statyi, pisma, vospominaniya* (Articles, Letters, Reminiscences) (Moscow: I.N. Kohlchev, 1907), 1:64.

11 Anon. "Ira Aldridge as Shylock," 839.

The most obvious and harsh attack came from the Slavophile camp. In the newspaper *Den'*, published by I.S. Aksakov, there was a "letter to the editor" titled "Aldridge-Othello" and signed by N. Kokhanovskaya (N.S. Sokhanskaya), a writer whose several novellas were being published alongside those of Turgenev, Goncharov, and others in the best periodicals of the 1850s. The writer was breathless with indignation:

Here is a pure Negro who is representing for us one of the deepest creations of Shakespeare's art. He is a Moor of Venice not only in the role he plays but also in his black skin....This is as close as possible to the truth, to the very source of sublime aesthetic pleasures! But *what is the truth*—at least, what is it when we talk about art, the greatest pleasure and expression of the human soul? The real truth of art is not in the external cover that we can touch with our hands....So they bring from overseas this apotheosis of Shakespeare's creation: not an invented but a real, exotic, black, natural-born Othello for us to see. And we saw him, but what exactly did we see? Raw flesh with earrings and shiny medals, shaming the spirit of contemporary art. And this disgrace is truly ours if we are ready to accept that Aldridge's blackness helps us to penetrate deeper and more fully into the spirit of Shakespeare's poetry. If lips are thick and dark blue, are they able to express better the cries of a human soul, cries emanating from the poet's universal soul? What happened is exactly what was supposed to happen because the flesh always impinges upon the spirit. The screams were wild and natural; the roars, the beastly howls, sounded like those of an animal that had been wounded; they were real lion-like sounds. It was as though this was not the Maly Theater in Moscow but an African jungle filled with shrieks coming from this powerful howling black flesh. It was this flesh that killed the spirit. Our aesthetic sentiment was mistaken in its expectations. It forgot that *it is the spirit that giveth life, the flesh profiteth nothing.* And to anyone who is sensitive to this spirit, this *natural*, black Othello, instead of great pleasure, offers nothing but—if you'll excuse me—disgust. (italics by Kokhanovskaya)

Kokhanovskaya's letter was not an accidental attack on the pages of a major Slavophile publication. I.S. Aksakov added his own "comment" to it in which he tried to support his opinion by quoting Schiller and Hegel: "The liveliness of Madame Kokhanovskaya's artistic impressions is fully justified in the following verse by Schiller:

Die Kunst soll nie die Wirkichkeit erreichen
Und siegt Natur, so muss die Kunst entweichen.

That is, art is never supposed to reach reality, and where nature takes the upper hand, there art must yield. Schiller's view was shared and developed by Hegel in his aesthetics. Our personal opinion is very close to that of Madame Kokhanovskaya as well."[12]

Kokhanovskaya's letter stated very clearly the contempt of a white slave-owner toward the Negro as a subhuman species of a lower race, an attitude well-known to Aldridge since his childhood. The letter provoked a storm of indignation. Vladimir Monumentov gave it a brilliant reproof in his "lyrical sketch" entitled "Aldridge in Moscow":

> *The editor's office. He is sitting at the table and reading* Shishkov's On Ancient and New Style. *Suddenly an associate runs in. She is pale. Her attire is disheveled.*

---

12 N.S. Kokhanskaya, "Aldridge-Othello" (letter to the editor), *Den'* (Day) 39 (September 29, 1862): 17-18.

ASSOCIATE:

I have torn my clothes to pieces.
I have put on those of mourning!
With all my inside I sobbed
Since seeing Aldridge as Othello!

>Now that I see the light again
>Of the mysteries of the Russian folk
>I really should have stayed home
>Under the skies of my native Ukraine!

>I would not have been able to see
>While consuming local dumplings,
>How this *black flesh*
>Is abusing the spirit in its fleshly way!

>I curse this black race
>That gave birth to Aldridge!
>But I am fainting…give me some cider!
>And wet my temples and forehead with whiskey!

She faints. The editor brings her round. She stands up and again begins her declamation.

>This disgraceful spectacle
>With my Byzantine brush
>I will paint swiftly for you:
>Here is a black body
>With earrings and medals all over it!
>*Fat lips—and dark blue too!*
>Where am I?—Am I at the Maly Theater?
>Or am I in an African desert?
>And hearing barbarian growls.
>I am trembling in fear (as I am a maiden),

I have understood these filthy screams:
This is the *war* of this militant *flesh*!

She steps forward. Her eyes are aflame glistening insanely.

Black body! Black skin!
Raw flesh in earrings in front of me!
Spirit is the life-giver,
Flesh is nothing!
Pour cider on my forehead! Ah!...

She faints again. The editor is supporting her."[13]

Kokhanovskaya was unanimously rebuffed by the progressive press. Neither she nor Aksakov risked attacking Aldridge in public again, but in their private correspondence they continued to exchange their characteristic opinions. Aksakov wrote to her in 1862, saying,

You have really been attacked for your Aldridge piece! In verse and in prose! In Moscow and in St. Petersburg papers! I am mad at myself for letting you publish that letter. Let anyone else, not you, try to curb this false delight of the public: you, as an artist, should stay outside of all debate, all the crush of the literary crowd. I never

---

13 Vladimir Monumentov, "Aldridge in Moscow. A Lyrical Scene," *Razvlechenie* (Entertainment) 41 (October 11, 1862): 190. Under the penname of Monumentov, the young V.P. Burenin was hiding. He was at that time a leader of the progressive camp who later became one of the most odious figures at *Nashe Vremya* and specialized in the defamation of the narodniks. Monumentov added a footnote to the sketch, saying, "All expressions printed in italics have been taken by us from the wonderful article by Madame Kokhanovskaya printed in *Den'*, No. 39."

saw Aldridge in *Othello* but I saw him in *Macbeth* and hated him, but I also saw him in *Lear* and, conversely, liked him a lot! This is understandable: in *Lear* he had to play a white, grey-haired old man and not give any freedom to his Negro nature, restrain it as much as possible, hide it—in a word, in this role he was not natural but he was an actor. It came out well because he is a remarkable and smart actor. The more contrary a role is to his nature, the more he can use makeup and hide his African looks, the better.

In other words, Aksakov did recognize a superb actor in Aldridge but with a reservation: he is superb only when he destroys his inborn "nature." Kokhanovskaya was a consistent follower of her editor but never modified her stance one bit:

> You are saying that I have been attacked for my Aldridge letter and regret that you gave me the chance to publish it....You should not regret it though! Being an artist, I had to contribute to the debate, as my artistic feeling was insulted by this black flesh and colorless spirit. I do not repent. For me my artistic feeling is my second conscience, and the disgust caused by Aldridge was so immense that I could only get rid of it through this public confession— and nothing else. But I will not take part in the pushing and shoving on the literary square, or display my wounded pride by replying to the poems and prose. I won't even consider it, simply because I have not even read them.[14]

---

14 Anon. "Correspondence of Aksakov with N.S. Sokhanskaya (Kokhanovskaya)," *Russkoe obozrenie* (Russian Review) 45 (1897): 530-31.

One of Aldridge's defenders, A. Ivanov (A.I. Urusov), appalled by the attacks of the reactionaries, wrote, "*Den'* and *Nashe Vremya* are treating Aldridge so savagely that the translation of these articles into a foreign language, say into English, would give the saddest idea about the state of our education."[15]

The young journalist was wrong: had Kokhanovskaya's review in English translation found itself in the hands of those numerous gentlemen with whom Aldridge had such sad interactions in North America and England, he would not have provoked anything in them save complete agreement and sympathy.

---

15 Urusov, *Statyi, pisma, vospominaniya*, 65.

ALDRIDGE IN THE PROVINCES

===============C3===============

*I*n the years 1861-1866 Aldridge toured Russia several times. One of the tours to Povolzhye and the central part of Russia lasted almost a year. Aldridge also toured the south of Russia, western parts, and Ukraine. He visited Rybinsk, Yaroslavl, Nizhny Novgorod, Kazan, Voronezh, Ryazan, Tambov, Penza, Novgorod, Kaluga, Samara, Saratov, Astrakhan, Kharkov, Rostov-on-Don, Kiev, Odessa, and Zhitomir. This list is not complete and could easily be doubled. None of the famous Russian actors, not even Shchepkin or Mochalov, were able to visit that many Russian towns. Aldridge's tours have been chronicled in a number of touching memoirs by fellow actors. He played an enormous role in the history of Russia's provincial theater.

His tours took place during a great social upsurge. Under the pressure of a growing peasant movement, the government had to emancipate the serfs in 1861. A new group of progressive readers and theatergoers had emerged from the educated classes (*raznochinetz* and *intelligentsia*). These new spectators were the ones who were behind Aldridge's special success in the provinces. Building on their sympathy, Aldridge could play a Shakespearean repertoire in towns that could not boast of any serious theaters. Aldridge did not bring his own troupe with him; he played with Russian actors from the local theaters and sometimes even with amateurs.

The provincial Russian theater of that period was leading a pitiful existence. Many troupes consisted of leftovers from the serf theaters that had disappeared due to the financial problems of their owners. For such actors, acting had always meant entertaining their master, who wrote his critical remarks with a whip across their backs. In Russia's provincial theater the age-old habits of slavery and absolute humiliation were still alive; actors felt they were the property of the theater owner or entrepreneur. They all were leading a miserable existence without rights or food and worked in horrible conditions. A small audience, consisting mainly of gentry, merchants, and government clerks, demanded that a new play be put on every day with no attention paid to the quality of production. This is why the artistic level of a provincial theater was very low. The repertoire included mainly vulgar comic operas and silly melodramas. No serious creative work on a play and no pursuit of serious artistic results were possible. As P.A. Strepetova recounts, "in the provinces there was the strongest bias against actors and against theater in general."[1] Only new spectators coming from the younger democratic generations had a yearning for good theater. But the provincial theater, backward and uncultured, could no longer satisfy these spectators.

Aldridge's emergence on the provincial stage was a major event. Of all the great actors in the world, Aldridge was the first to perform in Russia's backwoods, where no

---

1   P.A. Strepetova, *Vospominaniya i pisma* (Memoirs and Letters) (Moscow: Academia, 1934), 261.

European actor would ever set foot. Not only did he play well—he also taught Russian provincial actors, giving them an example of professional craftsmanship and familiarizing them with the achievements of European theater.

A memoir written by a contemporary about the Rybinsk theater gives an idea of the atmosphere in which Aldridge found himself touring the provinces. One V. Smirnov was the owner of the local theater. He received it as part of his wife's dowry, and, according to Strepetova, "understood virtually nothing in matters of art," but was well-informed about the matter of profits. He thought of himself as a director: "During rehearsals he maintained discipline; he yelled, reprimanded, ordered, but had nothing to do with the development of roles. He was solely concerned with actors knowing their lines, but how they performed was none of his business."[2]

"Salaries were no higher than 25 rubles a month! Which was not often the case; it was 8 rubles for the most part. Besides, there were several senile and alcoholic actors who would get a couple of rubles as tips when the boss was in a good mood. All the leading actors made money only on benefit nights and survived on gifts they got from spectators." At night destitute actors slept in the box-seats. Smirnov wanted them out of there, saying that "decent people complain that it is impossible to touch the elbow rests without being stung by various insects."[3] Such was the depressing atmosphere in which the world-famous actor had to play.

---

2   Ibid., 167-68. On Aldridge's collision with entrepreneur V. Smirnov, see Anon. "Biographical Anecdotes: Aldridge and Smirnov," *Souffleur* 75 (October 2, 1880).

3   Dalmatov, "Aldridge na yarmarke," 732.

Provincial actors initially did not really welcome Aldridge into their midst. The vicious rumor about his fiery temper, about him beating up his co-stars in fury, circulated widely among them. Aldridge's innovative techniques brought condemnation from conservative performers. And his overwhelming success also provoked their envy.

Occasionally there were schemes behind the curtains aimed at Aldridge and actresses who agreed to play opposite him as Desdemona. Actress A.N. Mochalova, who in her younger days in Odessa had played Desdemona at his behest, recalled,

> Then the murder scene ensued. After saying my prayers, I go to bed. Othello enters. Suddenly I feel that the bed boards underneath me are breaking; my legs are hanging through the boards. I instantly understood. "Someone has sawed them off; they want to damn this scene....If I fall through, there will be a scandal." And now Othello is all over me. I hold my breath. Instinctively I stretch out, press my feet and head against the ends of the bed. A moment later the boards give way. I look at Othello and whisper in horror, "Softer, softer!" He understood me. "A, racaglie!" he hissed, and continuing to act, he quickly pulled down the curtain above the alcove. A second later he reappeared on the steps, visibly shaken. The public did not notice anything. His face was terrible, however. The eyes blazed like those of a wolf. If at that moment he had seen any of my comrades who had contrived this trick, he would have strangled them. But the audience sat motionless with horror, seeing this tiger's face. The applause was endless.[4]

Aldridge often had to teach many of the provincial actors how to act, and he also gave lessons in theater

---

4 Verbitskaya, *Moemy chitateliu*, 15.

etiquette. He would begin by turning into a director for this crowd who did not know what a director was. At the first rehearsal he called the actors up and in a friendly manner addressed them by name, conversed with them in order to get to know them, and on parting said, "I hope to see you in the best of health." Such manners were unknown in the theater of that time.

Dalmatov remarks that

> at the beginning Aldridge's behavior on stage disappointed everyone. First, he muttered to himself, sometimes not even looking at his partner and not listening to him; secondly, he paused where appropriate to allow others to say their lines as though he understood what they were saying. He was very discreet, polite and helpful with fellow actors who always felt at ease toward the end of a rehearsal. He soon enchanted almost everyone, save one tragedian who was unhappy with his acting because Aldridge would not roar, scream or growl. The tragedian would get drunk, and when Aldridge was on stage, he would walk backstage and scream, "I am here, you Negro mug, come on out!" He was really appalled by the acting of this visiting artist: it broke all the traditions of the loud-voiced Karatygins.[5]

Good-natured in everyday life, Aldridge was a very demanding director. He insisted that actors know the text, think through their actions on stage, strictly observe the agreed blocking, and show consideration for the ensemble. But he was very friendly with fellow actors and always ready to help out in anything he could, explaining their roles and going through their lines. His explanations were always simple, precise and full. Russian actors who performed

---

5   Dalmatov, "Aldridge na yarmarke," 733.

alongside Aldridge learned for the first time what it was like to work for a director, and by following his instructions, they learned to respect the art in acting. Productions with his participation were the best ever in Russian provinces of the 1860s. One provincial actress recalled, "We respected him so much that we always studied our roles, and everything went so smoothly when he was in charge. Once it so happened that he forgot the book for the prompter; there was no time to go and get it, so we talked him into not worrying and played without the prompter!"[6] This was a great rarity at a time when the whole performance depended on the prompter.

The actors' complete ignorance of their roles and full reliance on a prompter were typical of the provincial theater to such a degree that before Aldridge's arrival in Saratov in 1864, a local newspaper published the following announcement addressed to P.M. Medvedev's troupe, one of the best in the provinces: "The troupe is facing a difficult task....We beg the actors to study their roles well, and for this one production not to rely on the prompter too much....The hardest part will fall to Aleksandrova who will have to play Cordelia, Lady Macbeth, and Desdemona." Alas, the actors did not respond to this appeal, and the very first performance showed their "unsatisfactory, hasty command of their roles, which impeded Aldridge's playing."[7] Wherever Aldridge found himself, time and again he had to pressure actors to memorize their parts and treat his directorial guidelines attentively. It was only due to his reasonable firmness and friendly camaraderie that he managed to achieve satisfactory results.

---

6   Yunge, *Vospominaniya*, 172.
7   V.M., "Feuilleton," 2.

Figure 7: Aldridge offstage

In P.M. Nadimova-Shamshenko's unpublished memoir, we find a curious account of Aldridge in Odessa:

> Aldridge arrived in our city in 1861. Playing in English, he performed in *Othello, Merchant of Venice, King Lear,* and a comic opera about a Negro servant—his whole repertoire, and was paid a third of the box-office returns. Prompting did not turn out to be as difficult as anticipated. One merely had to make certain notes in the text: if he gestures with his right hand or left, takes a few steps to the right or to the left, goes toward the back of the stage or comes forward to the proscenium—he would do exactly the same gestures and movements again, so the prompter always knew when to give the cue to the next actor; there would be no pause and no interruption of his soliloquy. As a result, he could play ten performances and everything would go smoothly, without any mistakes and misunderstandings.[8]

This story shows the naïve surprise of an experienced actor who for the first time saw Aldridge's professionalism as an artist, so uncommon in Russia. This kind of careful development of a role was new to such an actor, who had much to learn from the visitor. Aldridge remained sensitive and kind, fully aware of the hard life of Russia's actors.

Actor A.A. Alekseev once happened to meet Aldridge in Kiev, where they were both acting in the same theater:

> He and I alternated in playing, and it was clear that his performances drew in crowds, while my audiences were small. Conscious of my uselessness to the owner of the theater, I cancelled the remainder of my shows on

---

8 P.M. Nadimov-Shamshenko, "Vospominaniya Aktyora" (Memoirs of an Actor), Manuscript No. 1016. A.A. Bakhrushin Theater Museum, Moscow.

condition that the manager would grant me a benefit night to cover my expenses. The manager agreed and allowed me to stage whatever I wanted. I instantly approached Aldridge, requesting that he take part in my benefit. "All right," he said via an interpreter, "'I will play and even sing. I have a comic opera with me in which I play a Negro lackey. I already did it in St. Petersburg." — "Thanks very much," I replied gratefully. "And what are you going to sing?" — "I will add a Russian song, "Vo piru byla, vo besedushke" (During the feast, in the gazebo) that I learned a long time ago."

Aldridge's participation in the comic opera, and especially the song, attracted so many people that there wasn't a place in the hall for an apple to fall. Aldridge sang the song in comical manner; it was really hilarious. The audience encored endlessly. He sang the song more than ten times.[9]

What other touring tragedian would have agreed to interrupt his tour and come to the rescue of his competitor? There were countless benefit nights for provincial actors in which Aldridge took part. They brought in a lot of money but he never charged a kopeck for his performances. For all this, Russian provincial actors responded to him with warm love. Aldridge's influence was fruitful and lasting.

He also impressed provincial spectators. One of them gratefully noted in the mid-1860s, "For several years now Aldridge has been touring the country and enlightening Russian public about the immortal works of Shakespeare; currently there seems to be no provincial town, nor any local

---

9   A.A. Alekseev, *Vospominaniya Aktyora A.A. Alekseeva* (Memoirs of Actor A.A. Alekseev) (Moscow: Artist, 1894), 136-39.

fair, which the rays of Shakespeare's genius have not reached, thanks to the tragedian."[10]

Wherever he went, Aldridge always brought Shakespeare with him and attracted attention to him, raising the taste of the public to a level previously unheard of in the provinces. Even in Odessa, a half-European city, as its chronicler Aleksandr De-Ribas testified, there had been "no Shakespearean repertoire"[11] performed prior to Aldridge's arrival—smaller and more remote places notwithstanding. This was a new epoch in each town's cultural life.

What did Aldridge bring to the sad reality of the Russian provincial theater? This is answered in the memoir of another chronicler, from Nizhny Novgorod:

> Three or four weeks ago a rumor was spread around the city that Ira Aldridge, a renowned actor, is coming to visit us. At first we did not even believe it, knowing that our residents are completely indifferent to stage art. Why would this actor even bother to come here? In our imagination we saw empty houses, sleepy patrons who were probably asking themselves why a theater even exists in Nizhny Novgorod, sleepy performances of the actors, which were entirely appropriate considering that no one paid any attention to them, and sleepy coachmen waiting out back. So it felt like there was no way that someone like Aldridge could come here.
>
> But the rumor about Aldridge's arrival turned out to be true. When he first appeared on our stage as Othello, the theater was full. He deserves the glory and fame he has achieved for his artistic and inspired acting. Seeing

---

10 I. Goltz-Miller, "The Black Tragedian and the White Audience," *Odesskii Novosti* (Odessa News) 21 (February 3, 1866).

11 De-Ribas, *Staraya Odessa*, 121.

him as Othello or Lear or Macbeth is like seeing not Aldridge but Othello, Lear or Macbeth."[12]

Aldridge dispelled the sleepiness and boredom of this provincial city.

His performances were exceptionally successful; everywhere he had the same full houses that in 1864 he had in Kaluga where he "gave two performances, and despite the monstrously high price of tickets, they were all sold out."[13] In Saratov Aldridge's performances were sold out as five-show passes, and the house was full.[14] "Aldridge's stay

---

12 A.S. Gatsisky, *Nizhegorodski Teatr 1798-1867* (Nizhny Novgorod Theater 1798-1867) (Nizhny Novgorod: Tipografia Gubernskogo Pravlenia, 1867), 68-69. In N. Barsukov's "Nizhny Novgorod Notes," *Teatr* 5 (1939): 134-37, there is an account of Aldridge's stay in Nizhny Novgorod that is replete with numerous errors. For instance, the author claims that Aldridge was there in 1858 while in that year he was on tour only in St. Petersburg. Commenting on Aldridge's relationships with Shchepkin and Shevchenko, the author places them together in 1858 and claims, "In Nizhny Novgorod the great representatives of three nations met: a Negro tragedian, a Russian actor and a Ukrainian poet (137)." However, while Aldridge in fact did meet Shevchenko in December 1858, he first met Shchepkin in 1862 in Moscow. Shevchenko noted in his diary Shchepkin's stay in Nizhny Novgorod on December 24-29, 1857, but does not mention Aldridge there, as he was still in Germany at that time (see the book by N.M. Dobrotvor, *Taras Shevchenko v N. Novgorode: Spornik* (Taras Shevchenko in Nizhny Novgorod: A Collection) ([Gorky]: Gorky Regional Press, 1939), 92.

13 I.L. Batalin, "Theater of Kaluga," *Russkaya Stsena (The Russian Stage)* 12 (1864): 187.

14 Anon. *Saratovskie Gubernskie Vedomosti* (Saratov Provincial Gazette) 31 (July 11, 1864): 306.

in Kazan created a real coup." The theater was "too small to fit all the spectators." Twenty performances were given at double price with average takings of about 1000 rubles."[15] "Aldridge's arrival in Odessa (1866) set the whole theater world in commotion. Despite high ticket prices, the first performance drew a full house. Many people sold their tickets at five times the initial price; whole families bought boxes; a lot of tickets were sold well in advance."[16] The journal *Antrakt* (Intermission) in 1866 published the following note:

> Famed tragedian Aldridge is happy with the warm hospitality he received in Russia and does not want to leave the country despite an invitation from Drury Lane Theatre in London. Currently he is traveling in our western provinces with a Russian troupe (headed by Kostrovsky). Recently he was in Zhitomir and gave several performances there. Despite the high ticket costs, there was always a full house. The Zhitomir public, that includes many Jews, liked Shylock most of all. The tragedy was played three times there. Othello was given twice.[17]

One could continue this chronicle of Aldridge's success in Russia's provinces for many more pages.

All this success was well-deserved. Aldridge was able to use his enormous talent and craft to destroy all the barriers created by a foreign language between himself and his spectators and make his acting accessible to the Russian audiences. One report from Rostov-on-Don confirms this peculiarity of his talent: "The feelings of sadness, despair,

15 Anon. "Kazan," *Russkaya Stsena* (The Russian Stage) 4/5 (1865): 247-48.

16 Anon. "[Ticket Prices]," *Odesskii Novosti* (Odessa News) 12 (January 18, 1866).

17 Anon. "[Note,]" *Antrakt* (Intermission) 34 (September 4, 1866).

hatred, love, wrath, anger, and joy were rendered by Aldridge so beautifully and clearly to anyone that had he even played his roles in Chinese, it would have made no difference."[18] A similar reaction to Aldridge's tour is found in Penza:

> Since November 29 our theater has changed its character. Mr. Ira Aldridge produces the strongest impression on our public. His truly artistic acting, deep understanding of Shakespeare, striking mimicry, melodic voice, superb gracefulness of movements, and naturalness of manners put a spell on the audience, engaging them in the play.[19]

An indication of the public's great interest in Aldridge's performances was the fact that a single play could be staged twice or three times in the course of some ten days. For example, in Penza (December 1864) within one week there was *Macbeth*, a repeat of *Merchant of Venice*, another *Macbeth*, and then a third *Othello*, at the request of the audience.[20] A Penza chronicler remarked, "We are not going to talk about Shylock nor about the self-sacrifices of our small troupe, which had to set aside its pride in order to take part in the productions with this rare gem."[21] This theater historian understood a comparison to a world-renowned actor would be devastating to the local thespians.

Summarizing Aldridge's tour in Saratov, a local observer could not help comparing the craft of the visiting actor with the skills of local tragedians:

---

18 K. A., "Aldridge on the Rostov Stage," *Russkaya Stsena* (The Russian Stage) 8 (1864): 115.

19 Sokolov, "Penza Theater," 332.

20 Ibid.

21 Ibid.

Aldridge's appearance in provincial towns could not have gone unnoticed. Local actors had to learn from Aldridge that the art of acting was not in bull-like roaring or screaming but rather in capturing the essence of the passion in the play. Whether a tragedian is silent, or mumbling to himself, or making a movement, or speaking with his eyes—everywhere there must be passion in its many different shades. No doubt this is not easy, but one has to study hard to become a tragedian. The craft of acting is more than just fainting or emitting blood-curdling cries. There are some people who have argued that once upon a time Saratov had a dramatic actor better than Aldridge—Bobrov. He had a deep voice, huge spade-like hands, and he was also very tall. But "There is only one step from the great to the ridiculous," or so we thought as we watched the actors who played with Aldridge. He had to have a lot of patience to forget about those surrounding him. Thankfully, those who played with him remembered their lines, but in Astrakhan even that was not the case.[22]

In Tambov Aldridge was very popular, as attested by by the young V.N. Davydov, who took part in his productions. The residents there were so enthralled by his Othello, Lear and Shylock that they also wanted to see Macbeth, but the local troupe did not have the energy, space, or props to do it. Then amateurs volunteered to do it. An observer remarked that

> without their participation we would not have been able to see Macbeth with all its scenic difficulties. The most surprising thing was that, despite all this complexity, it took them only three days to prepare for the performance. Everything was done very tastefully. The amateurs promised a fixed amount of 300 rubles to Aldridge for his

22 A.I., "In Saratov," *Volga* 40 (September 5, 1864): 149.

role. Significant expenses included enormous costs for new decorations, military music, magic, etc. The amateurs may have been fearful that, despite costumes costing more than 500 rubles, they still might also end up having to pay Aldridge's salary from their own pockets. But, thanks to the huge turnout, these concerns were in vain. The takings were fabulous, amounting to 808 silver rubles, so that even after paying Aldridge as well as staging expenses of 425 rubles, 83 rubles and 39 kopeks remained. The profit was donated to Tambov's poor.[23]

The naïve excitement in this account is quite understandable. The Tambov observer is amazed by the singularity of what he is describing: this "amateur" *Macbeth*, with a great actor in the lead role, the riskiness of the whole venture, the speed with which it was done, and the unprecedented material gains. 800 rubles was a large gain for a provincial theater at that time.

Davydov remembered this performance:

The amateurs tried their best and, to tell the truth, this production was much better organized and better performed than any with the professionals. As a goodbye gift, Aldridge was given bread and salt on a silver dish, with a silver ladle in Russian style, and a handmade towel with national decorations embroidered on it. Responding to the greeting, he took the bread in his hands and pressed it against his heart, covering it with kisses. He also gave out a number of his lithographed portraits as souvenirs, all signed tenderly. For many years to come one could see these portraits hanging on walls and included in family albums in many provincial homes.[24]

---

23 Anon. "Aldridge in Tambov," 341.
24 Davydov, *Rasskaz o proshlom*, 104-5.

These stories are evidence of the warm connection formed between Aldridge and progressive members of his audiences. Similar accounts have survived in other provinces. Here is what happened in Kazan where Aldridge's audience included students:

> The younger generation received Aldridge with delight. After a benefit performance for the Dramatic Arts Club, the students gave him a bouquet tied with a blue ribbon, inscribed in Latin "to greatest tragedian of all time." After another production he was given a laurel wreath with the same inscription, only in Greek. In addition, a special delegation was formed to express their immense gratitude for the endless pleasure his acting had given them by revealing "the true beauty of Shakespeare's plays."
>
> Aldridge was touched by these expressions. "Believe me, gentlemen," he said, "your gift will always remain dear to my heart. I will treasure your ribbons with those wonderful words as tokens of your affection for me. Your flowers will always remind me of this happy day, and I will make sure I preserve at least one petal as a memento. It will bring back memories of my dear Kazan students." *Wir sind alle Studenten* (We are all students), he kept repeating.
>
> For the residents of Kazan Aldridge performed *Macbeth* and *Richard III*, plays that even St. Petersburgers could not see.[25]

Aldridge did not just introduce Russia's provinces to Shakespeare, he also showed them the real art of theater that can be created by the talent, ideas, and hard work of an actor, combined with the genius of a playwright. This combination had never been seen in Russian provinces before. A black man, whom many had refused to acknowledge as a human being, taught provincial theater

---

25 Anon. "Kazan," 247-48.

audiences an important lesson about humanity and enriched their lives by submerging them for the first time in the depths of beauty and truth that can be found in the works of Shakespeare.

ALDRIDGE AND RUSSIAN ACTORS

======================= ⋈ =======================

*I*n his travels throughout Russia, Aldridge met an array of wonderful actors, some of whom were approaching the end of their careers and others who were just starting out. Memoirs about these meetings help us understand better his artistry, his creative method, and his place amongst actors of his time. We remember the strong impression Aldridge made on I.I. Sosnitsky, a master of stage realism who was highly regarded by Griboedov and Gogol.

His friend and colleague, M.S. Shchepkin, a founder of Russian realism, was also captivated by Aldridge, and even though they met when Shchepkin was in his last years, the older actor helped the tragedian understand his craft. It was Aldridge who initiated the meeting by asking N.H. Ketcher, a translator of Shakespeare, to take him to Shchepkin's house.

> After greeting him, Aldridge asked the translator to inquire if this little fat man with kind eyes and a sly smile had seen his performances. Shchepkin responded that he had indeed seen him and that he found Aldridge to be a man of great talent. Having heard that, Aldridge bowed

low but then insisted that he comment critically on his acting. "Well, tell him then," Shchepkin replied quickly, "that I did not like the entire scene in Act 2 when Desdemona arrives. When the galley brings her, Aldridge strolls toward her, takes her hand, and calmly leads her to the front of the stage. How can this be possible?! He forgets that Othello is a Moor, that within him boils hot southern blood, and he has not seen his wife in a long time. He doesn't just love his wife, but is madly in love with her. And now that she is before him, an object of both love and lust, blood should be rushing to his heart, and he should run up to her like an animal, forgetting everything around him, seize her, crush her in his embrace, carry her to the front of the stage, and only then remember that he is a commander, and that many curious stares are directed at him. Tell him"—here Shchepkin jumped up from his chair in an burst of artistic passion—"that he must cover her with kisses, kiss her arms and legs; yes, and tell him that he should…" and here he made an energetic gesture that cannot be mentioned in print. Aldridge, having heard Ketcher's translation, smiled and bowed his head in agreement.[1]

According to M.V. Lentovsky, who was living at Shchepkin's house at the time, Aldridge "spent about an hour in his house, getting his stories across either by miming them or through an interpreter. In *Othello*, Shchepkin thought him umatchable. Sitting at the table, the two celebrities laughed a lot as they were singing the Russian folksong that Aldridge performed in his comic opera while playing the part of a servant named Mungo."[2] On October 2, 1862, Aldridge presented Shchepkin with a photo of himself

---

1   Koni, "Iz dalyokogo proshlogo," 97-98.

2   V.M. Leontovsky, "At M.S. Shchepkin's," *Moskovskie Vedomosti* (Moscow Gazette) 116 (1895).

in the role of Othello, with a personal inscription. That photo is now kept at the Bakhrushin Museum in Moscow.

Figure 8: Aldridge as Othello

167

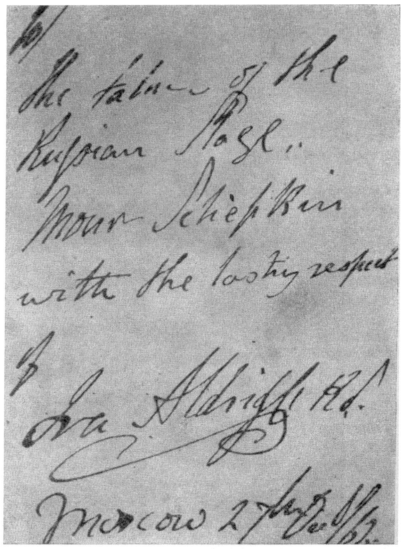

Figure 9: Aldridge's tribute to Mikhail Shchepkin

Actor A.A. Alekseev tells in his memoirs about Aldridge's meeting with another great realistic actor, Prov Mikhailovich Sadovsky:

Aldridge used to visit the Russian theater and was delighted by the acting of Sadovsky. At the same time, Sadovsky had a lot of respect for the tragedian as well. They were introduced to one another at an actors' meeting. Sadovsky ordered some wine. A translator took a seat with them, but Sadovsky shooed him away: "You, German, get lost," he said, "we will do fine without you."

And in fact they did! Sadovsky did not know a word of English, nor Aldridge Russian, but they sat together for a rather long time, and in the end were quite pleased with one another, although neither uttered a sound. They were just staring at each other intently. Once in a while Sadovsky would sigh deeply and nod his head, as though appreciating his talented crony—and Aldridge would do the same. Then Aldridge would grasp Sadovsky's hand firmly. The latter would reply in the same way. Then they would just smile at one another. And then more deep sighs, handshakes and smiles. Then they would silently wave their arms asking for more wine. The empty bottle would be replaced with a full one. Finally the silence was broken; they stood up, hugged three times, and parted.

An acquaintance stopped Sadovsky on the way out and asked him if he liked Aldridge and what they spoke about. "He is a good man," the actor replied, "very kind, but most importantly, not too talkative. I like that." Such a scene characterized better than anything else two artists by nature and not just by trade.[3]

Alekseev's naïve conclusion is not meaningless: Sadovsky and Aldridge knew each other's acting very well and could without words understand each other's artistic intentions.

Yunge's account of Aldridge's significance for the actors of St. Petersburg's Alexandrinsky Theater is very good:

---

3   Alekseev, *Vospominaniya,* 138-39.

In 1858 Aldridge's influence on our actors was enormous. Martynov, Maksimov, Sosnitsky, P.A. Karatygin, Grigoriev, Burdin, Leonidov—all of them were delighted by him and gave him standing ovations. Aldridge responded cordially. They confessed to him that they wanted to learn a lot from him, and in fact their acting did become simpler, livelier, and more thoughtful as a result.

Of them all, it was Martynov who was impacted the most. Our greatest comedian found his own true calling at that time and suddenly became a first-rate drama star. He was a true artistic genius who could shake people's souls. It was such a pity that Aldridge could not see him later in dramatic roles.[4]

After Aldridge's arrival, A.Ye. Martynov (1816-1860) lived for only two years, but it was in that brief period he suddenly showed his powerful dramatic talent. It was as though the touring tragedian had pushed the celebrated Russian comic toward a new path of drama. Soon after Aldridge's departure, Martynov created his inimitable Tikhon in *Groza* (The Thunderstorm). In the Ostrovsky play Martynov mastered the "art of shocking the audience" that Aldridge had achieved in Shakespearean tragedies.

Aldridge's influence on Russian actors who played Shakespearean roles was obvious almost immediately after his arrival. On November 25, 1859, L.L. Leonidov (1821-1889), a well-known tragedian widely regarded as a successor to V.A. Karatygin, played Othello in a new P.I. Weinberg translation and surprised most critics with his rejection of numerous techniques inherited from Karatygin. Leonidov played Othello

true to the central idea, with the sincerity and wholesomeness needed to play a simple, open, and strong

---

4   Yunge, *Vospominaniya*, 175.

character, with tender, passionate love and limitless jealousy dimming his reasoning, turning the skies dark, furious, and untamable. In places where Othello turns into a beast, one can see, in the horrific emotions he displays, his intense suffering and the torments that have crushed all his hopes. All this was visible in the performance of Leonidov, who had studied the role closely and played it without the slightest flaw.[5]

These lines do not leave any doubt that Leonidov modeled his Othello on Aldridge's interpretation and adopted his stage techniques. Critics openly acknowledged that "Leonidov for the most part very successfully followed Aldridge's example."[6]

Pointing to Aldridge's formative influence on many major actors in St. Petersburg, Yunge said, "Only V.V. Samoilov treated Aldridge with contempt and condescension, and this was rumored to be 'due to envy.' However, while loudly berating the African, he borrowed from his *Lear* probably more than anyone else and imitated him quite often."[7] One newspaper in St. Petersburg, not without Samoilov's own involvement, claimed his superiority over Aldridge as King Lear and even argued that Aldridge himself recognized that he was inferior to Samoilov in this role. But the observant and truthful Yunge suggested that in Samoilov's Lear one could clearly see borrowings from Aldridge.

---

5   A. G-fov, "Theater Chronicle," *Teatralny i Muzikalny Vestnik* (Theatrical and Musical Bulletin) 49 (December 13, 1859): 483.

6   Ibid., 461.

7   Yunge, *Vospominaniya*, 175.

Figure 10: Lithograph of Aldridge as Othello

Aldridge not only impacted major masters of Russian stage but also helped several beginners who later became successors to Shchepkin, Sadovsky, and Martynov. He helped bring to the stage such actors V.V. Charsky, P.A.

Strepetova, G.N. Fedotova, and V.N. Davydov. Charsky (184?—1910) as a young student was hugely impressed by Aldridge's acting. As I heard from the actor himself, this impression led him to embark on his 45-year-long career in theater. Charsky was a "very serious, university-educated person, with great erudition," N.N. Sinelnikov recalls. "When he finished his studies, he dedicated his life to acting: being madly in love with art, he knowingly chose a life full of obstacles and tests. He purposely avoided high society and gave his life to studying and performing the classics."[8] One of his major interests was playing Shakespeare's characters. Aldridge remained for him the ideal interpreter of these characters. My brother G.N. Durylin recorded Charsky's thoughts about Aldridge in 1907:

> Aldridge's acting made a terrifying impression. Actresses were afraid to play with him because he was so intimidating, and those who had to work with him could even forget their lines. He seemed so hot-tempered, but in reality was cool as the nose of a dog. He would be all smiles and laughs backstage shortly after a scene. Actresses playing Desdemona were really scared of playing the smothering scene as if it was real. Aldridge was surprisingly simple in his choice of costume: he always played Othello in a simple blue-striped canvas suit. I have never seen, nor ever shall see, another such Othello.

Charsky, by his own admission, borrowed heavily from Aldridge when working on Othello,

A very colorful account of meeting Aldridge was given by P.A. Strepetova (1850-1903):

---

8 Nikolai Nikolaevich Sinelnikov. *Shestdesyat let na Stsene. Zapiski* (Sixty Years on Stage. Notes) ([Kharkov]: Izdatelstvo Kharkovskogo gos. teatra russkoi dramy, 1936), 181.

I was eleven years old when Aldridge arrived in Nizhny Novgorod. I saw the tragedian-genius in *Othello, Macbeth,* and *Merchant of Venice,* and left the theater with many different impressions. Most of all I was taken, and probably not I alone, by his performance in *Othello.* I don't want to go into too much detail in talking about something so sacred that I keep deep in my soul.

Strepetova, a poor foundling adopted by a theater hairdresser, spent all her childhood backstage. She was fortunate to experience Aldridge's kindness firsthand. According to her, "he really loved children."

However, my bliss did not last long. Having finished his performances in Nishny, Aldridge left for Kazan. After his departure the box office receipts dropped; the theater looked deserted. God, how miserable and paltry did our local Nizhny celebrities seem to me now! "When am I going to see a good actor or actress again?' I thought to myself as I watched the howling of Mr. and Mrs. Trusov, or the clownish face of Madame Sakharova.[9]

This account shows us how Aldridge, a gifted actor, was able to reveal to talented people the artistic poverty of the Russian theater of the 1860s. He also gave future actors an example to follow. Neither Strepetova nor Charsky was destined to achieve the level of Aldridge's art, but within them forever lived a disdain for the mediocre provincial theater of their time.

Aldridge made an incredible impression on Glikeria Nikolaevna Fedotova (1846-1925). She had just turned sixteen when, after her successful debut at the Maly Theater in 1862, she saw Aldridge in his Shakespearean roles. A favorite pupil of Shchepkin and Samarin, Fedotova recalls in her memoir the strong impact Aldridge's acting had on her:

---

9   Strepetova, *Vospominaniya i pisma,* 54-55.

Some new, unfamiliar feelings came over me when I looked at Aldridge. He was black, unattractive, had a guttural voice, and played only in English, while our actors gave their lines in Russian, which really impeded the integrity of performances. But, despite all that, he made you forget everything and was so captivating, kind, naïve, and touching in his tender scenes and so scary and merciless in his furious ones. And yet I felt really sorry for this wonderful spirit, this great soul, as one would feel sorry for all Othellos, but this particular one was such an artless, helpless child of nature, devoid of worldly wisdom or cunning, that the grief of the spectators was inconsolable. There is nothing more tormenting than watching the sufferings of the helpless soul of an innocent child! He was such a superb tragedian.[10]

V.N. Davydov wrote, "Aldridge produced an enormous impression on me....His arrival turned my head completely, and my participation in one of his productions made me so busy with preparations and gave me so much trouble, even though I didn't have any lines." In that production the young Davydov observed Aldridge's hard work on his role and witnessed the amazing results. Aldridge's performances convinced Davydov of the limitless strength an actor at the height of his powers had over his audiences.

It was an eye-opener for me regarding the art of acting. Much later, when I became an actor myself, the example set by the black tragedian proved to be the main guideline for my work, for my school. I realized that everything in this art has to be strictly and precisely worked out. This was the alpha and omega of stage art. Inspiration, enthusiasm empower the actor on stage, his temperament

---

10 Unpublished notes of G.N. Fedotova. I am deeply thankful to G.I. Goyan for permitting me to use this excerpt from Fedotova's autobiography.

makes his characters animated and convincing, but only hard preparatory work will give him the chance to truly create, to control every gesture, every turn, every sound of his voice in front of the audience. This peculiarity, to control and create simultaneously, is key to the true art of the theater....

Many believe that Aldridge was mainly an actor of instinct, judging by his great stage sensitivity. There were conversations about this sensitivity: his capacity to react acutely and deeply to everything while acting, being such that he would forget about the actors who played with him and indeed had wounded several of them, and had almost strangled several Desdemonas. These are all tall tales generated by the yellow press and the shallow public. As far as I remember the tragedian's acting, Aldridge's art had all the signs of huge preparatory work, while his ability to control was exceptional.

Davydov, who himself created a whole school of acting and influenced several generations of Russian actors, regarded Aldridge's contribution to Russian theater very highly:

Aldridge was an actor who brought in novelty. For instance, he would do certain scenes standing with his back or half-face to the audience, which our actors had avoided; he also introduced a lot of minute nuances into his speech, spoke in an undertone, delivered certain scenes in a whisper, almost in one breath; used his movement throughout the stage, not just on the proscenium. It was hard for him to play with our actors. But he patiently explained things to them, via an interpreter, gave them pieces of advice, and whenever things went smoothly, rejoiced as if he was a child. He slapped himself on the hips and said goodheartedly, "Ochen khorosho, ochen spasibo" (Very good, very thank you!)

Davydov concluded that "He was a great tragedian, an actor whose analytic, preparatory skills were combined wonderfully with synthetic, truly creative work done in front of the public."[11] These words of the great master of Russia's theater contain an apt characterization of Aldridge as an artist and an actor.

An accidental visitor from afar, Aldridge did a lot for the Russian theater: his example showed that inspired work is the true foundation for real art, that an actor's talent, combined with enlightened effort, can produce a result that an audience cannot ignore. Aldridge conquered the Russian theater by the truth of his craft and became a comrade and teacher of Russian actors—from the great Martynov to any unknown toiler on a provincial theater. Aldridge proved that in the art of acting, free thought and heightened emotions could co-exist. He called for liberating the actor from all possible restraints that limit his freedom. This is why he provoked obstinate enmity from some and even more passionate affection from others. From the warm love of Shevchenko, Shchepkin, Sadovsky, Martynov, Davydov, Fedotova, and from appreciative Russian audiences, a timeless wreath was woven for Aldridge. This wreath will always lie on his forgotten grave at a cemetery in Poland, where this tireless wanderer had perished, killed by an illness on July 26, 1867, on his way to his beloved Russia.

A great actor forgotten by historians of American and European theater, Aldridge will always occupy a special honorary place in the history of Russian theater.

Let us think about the tragedy of Aldridge's personal life. An African by birth, he had to act in English, not in his native tongue. A great scholar and performer of Shakespeare, he could not make a career for himself in the homeland of the great playwright. All his life he had to travel from one place to another, knock on doors of foreign

---

11 Davydov, *Rasskaz o proshlom,* 101-3.

countries, foreign theaters. By historical chance, he had his greatest success in Russia, which he first visited when it was still a country of white slaves. It was here, in Russia, that he found like-minded people and admirers because his art and fate were similar to those of a number of talented actors of common origin, such as Shevchenko, Shchepkin, or Sadovsky. His art had the same truth of life in it, the same drive for freedom so familiar and dear to the Russian audience .

What a vast difference between the fate of the black actor and the life of Soviet actors! Our actors at national theaters do not have to run away abroad in order to act in a foreign language. They freely develop their own ethnic theaters and their own national cultures. *Othello*, for instance, is performed in the USSR in tens of languages—in the Caucasus, in Kirghizstan, in Kazakhstan, Uzbekistan, Tatarstan, and Bashkortostan. But this is not all: ethnic theaters annually demonstrate their accomplishments in the capital—in Moscow—and are greeted here with the brotherly hospitality of Russian actors and spectators. In the summer of 1935 Moscow saw a beautiful performance of *Othello* by the Bashkir State Academic Theater. In 1936 the Uzbek State Drama Theater presented its *Hamlet* to Moscow, with people's artist Abrar Khidoyatov playing the lead. The production of *Othello* by the Rustaveli Georgian Theater (Tbilisi), led by people's actor A.A. Khorava, received wide acclaim.

I think that there is one actor who, impressed by the rendering of Shakespeare in the languages of people oppressed by tsarist Russia and freed by the Soviet authorities, would have really appreciated these performances of *Othello* in Georgian or Uzbek. His name is Ira Aldridge. What he would have seen in Soviet Moscow or

Bukhara or Ufa or Yerevan would have been his dream come true, a completion of his fight for the rights of people of any race or nationality to develop world-class art and culture. This is why Ira Aldridge, who had experienced the persecution, contempt and slander of "enlightened" America and Europe, and still was able to make a great contribution not only to Russian culture but to the culture of the whole world, is so dear to our hearts. Were he alive today, he would be with us in our fight for a new global theater of liberated mankind.

Figure 11: Sergei N. Durylin

SERGEI NIKOLAEVICH DURYLIN

═ ═ ═ ═ ═ ═ ═ ═ ═ ═ ═ ═ ═ ═ CB ═ ═ ═ ═ ═ ═ ═ ═ ═ ═ ═ ═ ═ ═

Sergei Nikolaevich Durylin is considered by many as one of the creators of theater studies as a scholarly discipline. Before him there had been just reviewers, observers, and critics. However, theater became his primary focus after 1933, when he was around fifty years old. Why and how did this happen? Before that, albeit a theater admirer throughout his life and an avid theatergoer, he had never professionally done theater studies. But let us recount the whole story in due order.

It is hard to write a smooth, linear biography of Durylin, as he was a man of many talents, passions, and enthusiasms. Also, certain external circumstances break his life into separate periods that often do not have a clear-cut dividing line in between. The scope of his professional interests was broad: a literary critic, a theater scholar, an ethnographer and archaeologist, a religious thinker, philosopher, prose writer and poet, art critic—in all of these fields he left behind profound, groundbreaking works that are still in demand.

Sergei Nikolaevich was born into a merchant's family and brought up in the Orthodox tradition. His studies at the fourth men's gymnasium (from 1897) brought about his protest against the dry formalism of a public school system in which free thought and the creative will of the students were stifled. In 1904 he dropped out from middle school, feeling that it was impossible for him to continue when popular masses had no such opportunity. This was six years before his father had gone bankrupt and died, and the family had been ruined financially. Sergei began giving private lessons. He expressed his attitude toward the education system in the article "In the School Prison: A Student's Confession," released as a brochure by the publisher *Posrednik* in 1907 and then reissued in 1907 after a host of good reviews.

He emerged from the gymnasium having lost faith in God. Atheism and an acquaintance with adult revolutionary activists brought him to revolutionary circles. For these activities he was arrested many times and on three occasions spent several months in jail. The 1905 Revolution, followed by bloody reprisals against the revolutionaries, and the death of a close friend (a member of a militant unit) killed by gendarmes in 1907, made him think of the rationale of those sacrifices and whether the truth they tried to bring to the people was indeed the right answer. As a result of a painful spiritual crisis, Durylin arrived at the conclusion that no violence could be justified. And he would retain this conviction throughout his lifetime.

Years of anguished ruminations about the meaning of life, his place in it, and a search for his own path ensued. All that was beautiful and significant in the world had been created by those who "took their *own* path, their *own* risks, on their *own* feet. Each person has his own true and precise compass—his own self; and if he does not follow it just once, there will be no end to his wanderings." Once he realized this in 1907, Durylin never again lost this compass and continued pursuing his own interests despite all of life's cataclysms.

Presently Durylin began educating himself: in the library he studied books on literature, art, philosophy, and history. The Tretyakov Gallery became his arts academy. Apart from that, Durylin considered the Maly and Art (Khudozhestvenny) Theaters as his universities, in which he had admittedly obtained the education that gave "extremely much both to the mind and heart, to civic awareness and to thought." As a result, Durylin became a person of encyclopedic learning. His memory skills were phenomenal.

In 1905 Durylin began working for the publisher *Posrednik* that published works of Leo Tolstoy (1828-1910). Here the atmosphere of lofty thinking reigned supreme, and everything was saturated with the influence of Tolstoy's personality. Soon Durylin became secretary of a journal published by *Posrednik* called *Svobodnoye Vospitanie* (Free Upbringing). Here he studied the experience of the most progressive schools of Europe, Russia, and America, and wrote a host of articles on pedagogy without leaving his own teaching practice.

In response to Durylin's claim that a pedagogue also needs freedom, Tolstoy said, "Freedom always is for something and from something....One can use it to any kind of ends. True freedom is possible only if one observes the moral law. *Only a religious person is a free person*" (my italics—V.T.). A few years later Durylin arrived at the same conclusion and would stick to this principle in his teaching practice.

His talent as a pedagogue attracted students to him throughout his life. Many of them later became well-known people, scholars, and actors. He was gratefully remembered in print by such actors as Igor Ilyinski (1901-1987) and

Mikhail Nazvanov (1914-1964), and by literary scholar and poet Tyutchev's great-grandson Kirill Pigaryov (1911-1984). Poet Boris Pasternak (1890-1960) admitted that it was Durylin who introduced him to literature.

In 1909 Durylin paid a visit to Tolstoy in Yasnaya Polyana and received his praise. During this visit, Durylin was enchanted by Tolstoy's personality and retention of "some sort of non-resistance for good" in his soul. His conversations with Tolstoy about the religion of love, about the moral religious consciousness that could prevent people from committing atrocities and violence, about the fact that one needs to study one's soul, train one's mind to be cautious in judgments and one's heart to be peace-loving, would occupy Durylin's thoughts for a long time to come and help him resolve anguished meditations on "what the truth is" and what his own destiny in life was.

1910 was a breakthrough year for Durylin by his own admission: "I came back to the faith of the fathers." That year new books turned up on his working table: hagiographies and works by the fathers of the church. He read the book *Life of St. Francis of Assisi* by Paul Sabatier (1858-1928) and *Easter Letters* by Vladimir Solovyov (1853-1900). Both books had a great influence upon him. Atheism and the noisy nihilism of those around him were counter to what was going on in his soul. His God was a God who was "quiet, not demanding talks and arguments. Only silence and peace." In one of his letters from that period he wrote, "Despite my far from peaceful younger days, despite all my passions, despite—and this is not an overstatement—all my sins, I have always sought and am still seeking inner religious humility. I am a peaceful and peace-loving person."

In 1908 Durylin began to attend lectures at the Archaeological Institute, and in 1910 he was admitted to its correspondence division, having chosen the history of literature and art as his specialization. He had to borrow forty rubles from several friends for an initial tuition payment. His choice of this particular institute was apparently caused by his love of the Russian North, Russia's antiquity, and his bent for traveling. Durylin traveled almost every year either by boat or on foot, alone or with a geological party on the institute-sponsored research trips: in 1906, 1908, 1911, 1914, and 1917 in the North; in 1909-10 along the Volga and Kama, and among ancient Russian towns. He recorded some northern folklore—folksongs, fairy tales, oral accounts by the locals—and produced sketches of the architecture of local churches and descriptions of the peculiarities of their décor. Based upon these travels, Durylin published a number of works: "Behind Meridional Sun. Around Lapland On Foot and By Boat" (1913), "Ancient Russian Icon-Painting and Olonets Region"(1913), "Kandalaksha's Babylon" (1914), "Under the Northern Sky: Essays on Olonets Region" (1915). In 1913 the general assembly of the Society for Olonets Region Studies elected him a full member of their Society.

In 1908 Durylin became a member of a circle with the strange name of "Serdarda." It consisted of young poets, musicians, artists, and philosophers. "Here they recited poetry, painted, philosophized, had snacks, and drank tea with rum," Pasternak recalled in his essay "People and Positions."[1] Pasternak would greet everyone arriving at the start of the soiree by improvising on the piano. In an easy, good-spirited environment, gloomy thoughts disappeared

---

1 B.L. Pasternak, *Izbrannoye* (Selected Works) (Moscow: Chudozestvannaya Literatura, 1985), 2:245.

and a creative atmosphere reigned here: conversations about literature, music, art—everything a soul can crave.

Durylin's friendship with Pasternak lasted forty-six years. They both had a deep understanding of the soul and an appreciation of the creative essence of one another. Durylin called their relationship a "brotherhood of thought and heart."

Durylin was a contributor to the Symbolists' publisher *Musaget* throughout the period of its existence from 1910 to 1917. The *Musaget* publications included works by a large number of major philologists, historians of philosophy, literature, and the arts. Durylin was attracted by the fact that *Musaget* sponsored a series of lectures on the history of ancient Greek poetry, pre-Socratic philosophy, nineteenth-century French poetry, the history of German romanticism, and Russian lyricism of the nineteenth century. The aesthetics of Johann Wolfgang von Goethe (1749-1832) as well as the works of Richard Wagner (1813-1883), French Symbolists Charles Baudelaire (1821-1867) and Paul Verlaine (1844-1896), were also studied there. Durylin was attracted by the fact that symbolism was considered there not only as a poetic method but also as a "special mode of thought, an integral and harmonious theory of cognition." The moving spirit behind all these undertakings was Andrei Bely (1880-1934), an irrefutable authority of the circle in those days.

The 1911 *Anthology* released by *Musaget* included Durylin's poems along with the poetry of Alexander Blok (1880-1921), Maximilian Voloshin (1877-1932), A. Bely, Marina Tsvetayeva (1892-1941), Nikolai Gumilev (1886-1921), and Vyacheslav Ivanov (1866-1949). In the 1910s Durylin wrote, as he himself put it, "smooth symbolist verses and Franciscan sonnets." Under the penname of Sergei Raevsky, Durylin published three sonnets dedicated to St. Francis of Assisi in the *Anthology*. The medieval ascetic's deep influence on Durylin never subsided later in his life. Durylin also attended the Society for Free Aesthetics founded by Valery Bryusov (1873-1924), which met at the Literary and Artistic Circle directed by Bryusov.

As a participant of the Wagner circle, in the autumn of 1911 Durylin gave a paper on "Richard Wagner and Russia. About Wagner and Future Paths for Art." As he was delivering it, composer R.M. Glyer (1875-1956) played fragments of Wagner's operas *Lohengrin* and *Parsifal*, along with N.A. Rimsky-Korsakov's (1844-1908) opera *The Legend of the Invisible City of Kitezh and the Maiden Fevroniya*. E.K. Metner (1872-1936), *Musaget*'s publishing director, published Durylin's paper in a separate edition in the spring of 1913. In this work Durylin expressed his enthusiasm for Wagner's "myth-thinking." In addition, Durylin felt akin to Wagner's striving for a synthesis of music, word, and stage action subordinated to a single dramatic design. This would be reflected in his later oeuvre, particularly in his works on drama and its stage implementations.

In 1910 Durylin began frequenting meetings of the Moscow Religious and Philosophical Society in Memory of Vladimir Solovyov (RPS), and in 1912 he became RPS's Secretary, remaining as such until the Society closed down in 1918. Here he gave a number of presentations and socialized with all the cream of Russia's philosophical thought at the time: S.N. Bulgakov (1871-1944), N.A. Berdyaev (1874-1948), Ye.N. Trubetskoy (1863-1920), Ellis (1879-1947), V.F. Ern (1882-1917), Rev. Pavel Florensky (1882-1937), V.A. Kozhevnikov (1852-1917), I.A. Ilyin (1883-1954), and S.L. Frank (1877-1950).

Durylin's lectures in the 1910s were attended by the artist Mikhail V. Nesterov (1862-1942). Their personal friendship was initially established in 1912-13 and later grew into a very close companionship that lasted until the artist's death. Durylin never missed a single exhibition of Nesterov's paintings. Having once attended his personal exhibit in 1907, Durylin strongly recommended it to another friend sharing his rapturous impressions: "Some kind of a tender haze of childishly profound thinking envelopes all Nesterov's paintings. His *Holy Russia* and *Dimitrii, the Murdered Tsarevich* are striking....His Christ is ours, it is a national, Russian Christ." It was then that Durylin began collecting materials about Nesterov's creative work. He did not think about writing a book about him yet. He just decided to do it for himself, to create a collection of his favorite artist.

In 1913 the publishing house *Put'* (Path) invited Durylin to write a monograph on Nikolai S. Leskov (1831-1895): "Leskov: Personality, Legacy, Religion." It would take him years to write the book but it would never be published. The third part of the book, "Religion," was never to be completed. Durylin worked on Leskov until the end of his life, gave several presentations on him, but never managed to publish any of these studies. In the 1930s he would remark bitterly: "I worked on this monograph in 1914-15. The War intervened and then the revolution cut it short forever. [The book] will never be completed and will never leave the walls of my room."

Durylin's work as a literary critic began in 1908 when he published an essay on V.M. Garshin (1855-1888) "Khudozhnik-pravednik" (Artist-Righteous Man), in the journal *Svobodnoye Vospitanie*, No. 9. As a literary scholar, Durylin was interested in writers whom he could approach through his own method of seeking what was "characteristic of the personality and religious creativity" of the artist. He produced studies of M.Yu. Lermontov (1814-1841), Leskov, N.V. Gogol (1809-1952), F.M. Dostoevsky (1821-1881), Garshin, K.N. Leontiev (1831-1891), F.M. Tyutchev. He also gave lectures and wrote articles on I.V. Kireevsky (1806-1856), A.S. Khomyakov (1804-1860), Yu. F. Samarin (1819-1876), the Aksakov brothers. Lermontov became a focus throughout Durylin's life. His enthusiasm for this author was first born when he was a first-grader in primary school, and his parents presented him with a volume of Lermontov's poetry. That book can now be found on his working table next to the inkpot and kerosene lamp with a green lampshade in the Durylin Memorial House Museum in Bolshevo near Moscow. The list of Durylin's published literary studies and articles would take several pages. It could be complemented with works from his archives that were never published in the Soviet period due to censorship and concerns for his personal safety.

In the 1910s Durylin frequented the Circle of Seekers of Christian Enlightenment in the Spirit of the Orthodox Church. The Circle was not large in number. It united strictly Orthodox theologians, church figures, philosophers, and other scholars in a communal experience of God and spiritual communication. The Circle's organizer and moving spirit was Mikhail A. Novosyolov (1864-1938), a religious enlightener and publisher of a popular series called *The Religious and Philosophical Library*. The other members referred to Novosyolov deferentially as Avva-Mentor. *The Religious and Philosophical Library* series was a notable phenomenon in the life of the Silver Age intelligentsia. Its authors were mostly the Circle's members. Durylin's work was published twice: *Nachalnik tishiny* (The Chief of Silence, 1916) and the novella *Zhalostnik* (The Pitiful One, 1917). Political issues were not discussed at the meetings. The main task was the churching of Russian society that was supposed to occur not via reforms and agitation but through inner personal change on the basis of Christian enlightenment and studies of the foundations of the Holy Fathers' covenant. Novosyolov thought that it was only "the religious personality that could yield a social order that would retain both the high ideals and necessary social discipline." Berdyaev called this circle the "core of Russian Orthodoxy,"[2] while Florensky called it a "spiritual laboratory."[3]

Sergei Durylin's spiritual pursuits invariably led him to the Church. However broad the range of his interests and studies was, his path was strictly defined. It was quite logical that this path included his appearance in the Optina Hermitage (Optina Pustyn)—a male monastery in Kaluga region that was one of the centers of spiritual life in Russia. Durylin first visited Optina elder Anatolii (Potapov, 1855-1922) in late May of 1913 with his mother. "The nature in the Optina Hermitage is wonderful: solemnly quiet, *understanding*, submissive and sacred....This is a place created by a prayer that was briefer and more effective: it was easier for the lips to pronounce the most difficult words—those of humility, simplicity, and helplessness." The elder became Durylin's spiritual father, and without his advice Sergei Nikolaevich would never undertake any serious step.

On August 1, 1914 the war with Germany started. Durylin was not conscripted due to his myopia. In Moscow, Rybinsk, and Kostroma he delivered lectures on "Russia's Face. The Great War and Russia's Vocation" (he published a

---

2   N.A. Berdyaev, *Samopoznanie* (Self-Cognition) (Moscow: Eksmo 2006), 217.

3   P.A. Florensky, "Correspondence with M.A. Novosyolov," *Rev. Pavel Florensky's Archives* (Tomsk: Vodolei, 1998), 2:24.

book under the same title in 1916). He argued that "Russia is now *universally* pure, sacred and right. Germany is *universally* sinful and ruinous." In defining his motherland, Durylin now distinguished between *Russia* and *Rus*. At the time when *Russia* in these evil times "desperately clings to the newspaper, to the military telegram from the Supreme Commander, to the rumor about how much shrapnel has been manufactured, *Rus* leans to the prayer, to...the Optina Hermitage, to God."[4]

After the February "bourgeois" revolution of 1917 that temporarily liberated the Church from secular power, Durylin took an active part in church life: in pre-synod discussions, in organizing church brotherhoods. On August 15, 1917 the meetings of the All-Russian Synod of the Russian Orthodox Church in 1917-18 began. The Synod restored the institution of patriarchy abolished by Peter the First. The holy Patriarch of Moscow and All Russia elected by the Synod was Tikhon (Belavin, 1865-1925), who had previously been the Metropolitan of Moscow.

Durylin was invited to take part in the work of the Synod. He wrote about the synod in detail in his diary titled "The Olonets Notes."[5] Here we find his thoughts and concerns about the fate of the Church and Russia, the role of the intelligentsia and its relations with the Church, and the fate of Russian culture. Durylin actively published his articles in a new religious journal *Renaissance* (1918). At theology training courses he gives a series of lectures on "Religious Meaning in Russian Icon-Painting."

---

4   S.N. Durylin, *Rus prikrovennaya* (The Secret Rus) (Moscow: Palomnik, 2000), 291, 333.

5   S.N. Durylin, "From the Olonets Notes," *Nashe Nasledie* (Our Legacy) 100 (2011): 133-55.

The events of October 1917, when the Bolsheviks came to power and took ensuing repressive actions, signaled the end of Durylin's previous life. After 1918 we do not find in his diaries and notebooks any references to political events and his reactions to them. Durylin felt a barrier had emerged between himself and political reality. His subtle, impressionable soul could not withstand tumultuous, painful emotions and ruminations. He wanted to fence himself off from the outer world, to lock himself inside the "four walls."

Durylin sought salvation from the nightmarish situation in the country in his Church and his faith. His perception of the catastrophe coincided with the way it was depicted by Russian émigré intellectuals. Durylin never left Moscow; he saw and experienced everything; he was able to understand and anticipate many things. But he was unable to leave Russia: "I can only breathe Russian air."

The hopes for the reconstruction of the independent Church collapsed. In 1918 Durylin found himself lost in life: "I am in some sort of a circle that I cannot escape." He was more and more inclined to take religious vows. In 1919 Durylin lived in Sergiev Posad, next to the Troitsko-Sergieva Lavra near Moscow. As he prepared himself to taking the vows, he led a half-monastic life. However, he understood that he loved life, his people, and art too much, and he wanted to write prose. Meanwhile, monasteries were being destroyed by the Bolsheviks, and churches were shut down. Anatolii, the Optina elder, did not give his blessing for Durylin to take the vows. In 1920 Durylin accepted the advice of his spiritual fathers and became a priest serving at the Moscow church of Sacred Nikolai in Klenniki. The church's senior priest was Aleksii Mechev, who later would be canonized. Father Aleksii became Durylin's main spiritual supporter, teacher, and mentor. Durylin would later write warm, heartfelt memoirs about Father Aleksii and Anatolii, the Optina elder.

Persecution of the Church and its clergy affected Durylin as well. On July 12, 1922 he was arrested and charged with being a "politically harmful element by the Soviet authorities." Had he stayed in Moscow, he "would have continued his counterrevolutionary activities using his extensive connections with the world of reactionary clergy." Having spent several months in Vladimir's jail, Durylin was exiled to the city of Chelyabinsk for two years under the open surveillance of the OGPU (United State Political Department, predecessor of the KGB). He was facing a much more severe punishment, but his numerous friends and spiritual children successfully petitioned for a softening of his lot. Aleksii Mechev, being aware of Durylin's total inability to organize his everyday life, and understanding that without care he would die in exile, gave his blessing to Irina Alekseyevna Komissarova (1899-1976), his church's parishioner, to join him there: "Go with him, help him – people need him."

In Chelyabinsk Durylin was offered a job at the local folklore museum. He created an archaeology and ethnography department and headed it; he organized excavations at local mounds. At the same time he continued his literary scholarship and wrote novellas and short stories as well. He completed the initial two chapters (of fourteen in all in the final version) of his magnum opus, *In My Own Corner*.[6] He wrote a novella *Sudar' Kot* (Sir Tomcat), dedicating it to Nesterov. He wrote the initial three hundred

---

6   S.N. Durylin, *In my Own Corner* (Moscow: Molodaya Gvardia, 2006). This 879-page book was initially published in 1991 in an abbreviated form.

pages of a book on Nesterov, beginning it with a cycle of paintings about the Rev. Sergii of Radonezh. The OGPU asked to inspect this manuscript, but returned it after a while, probably finding nothing anti-Soviet in it.

Nesterov, a strict, severe judge, approved of the first chapter sent to him for feedback: "This is not just generalization about such a passé topic as Nesterov but a deep, emotional, heartfelt analysis which is not even impeded by your partiality to the author. Your religious experience…gives you the strength, persuasiveness, and novelty of authority that have previously been lacking in writings on me." In the same letter, dated March 17, 1924, Nesterov explained why he wanted Durylin to write a book about him: "I am really spoilt among all my fellows! In you I have not only a contemporary author but also a poet who is acutely sensitive to life, beauty, the soul of nature and man, and their great place in being. In you I have simultaneously a scholar and a theologian equipped with all the necessary traits to produce a complete work."[7]

It was only in 1949—seven years after the artist had died—that Durylin managed to publish the book, *Nesterov the Portraitist*. But his main monograph, *Nesterov in Life and Art*, remained a manuscript until 1965, when the publisher *Molodaya Gvardia* released it as part of the series *Lives of Remarkable People* (ZhZL), thanks to the great efforts of the publisher's editors.

On October 31, 1924 Durylin received an official note about the termination of his administrative exile. Now he could return to Moscow. Durylin was full of hopes and creative plans. He did not know that fate would allow him just two and a half years before another arrest. Church service as a clergyman was no longer possible. Though he

7   M.V. Nesterov, *Letters* (Leningrad: Iskusstvo, 1988), 296.

could not serve any more, he never left the Church. In that period, secret clandestine priests and monks were not uncommon.

1926 was the year of an important event for Durylin— M.V. Nesterov painted his portrait, a project that had been conceived back in 1922. Durylin's arrest and exile delayed carrying it out for four years. The portrait was titled *Difficult Thoughts*. Clad in a priest's cloak, with a crucifix seal ring, Durylin is sitting at a table over a sheet of paper, and his look is thoughtful and sad.

Figure 12: Portrait of Durylin by Mikhail V. Nesterov

Both the portrait and its title reflected Durylin's inner state. This was a time of painful thoughts about his future destiny, about the path fate had in store for him, about his place in this new life, and about himself, about who he was at the moment. He could not profess religious service now. Should he teach? But divinity schools had been shut down; religion as a subject had been eliminated. And the OGPU could not forget about his existence. "I am feeling amazingly unneeded." His studies of religion in the works of Gogol, Leskov, Dostoevsky, Lermontov, Leontiev, and Tolstoy were no longer possible.

On June 10, 1927 he was arrested again. This time his friends instantly began to intercede but to no avail. After five months in the Butyrskaya jail, he was exiled to Siberia. In the town of Tomsk, where he was followed by his spiritual daughter Irina Komissarova, his life was hard. Due to a secret OGPU ban, he was not allowed to get a job. Such was the way in which "politically unreliable" Durylin was deprived of any opportunity to make a living. He became a dependent, which was painful for him. Cold rented rooms, where snow could blow in through the holes in winter, want of money, frequent illnesses—all these would have ruined Durylin had he not had Irina's permanent care and support. She nursed and treated him, made the rooms habitable in winter, sewed clothes, nailed together bookshelves for the books their friends sent, ran around the town looking for writing paper, spun wool for socks and mittens on a self-made spinning-wheel, and annually carved a Russian Ded Moroz (Santa Claus) out of wood for New Year parties. She had no time to take care of herself but dedicated herself fully to Sergei Nikolaevich. She slept on a table, as there was no room for another bed.

Naturally, friends and spiritual children did not leave him in difficulty. They sent money, medicines, books; artists sent their paintings. Everyone was trying to support him materially and morally. Aware that correspondence was controlled by the OGPU, rare visitors brought letters and parcels with them. They kept him informed about cultural life in Moscow, especially the new theater releases. They tried to arrange for his articles to be published under pseudonyms and brought him his honoraria. For instance, N.N. Gusev, Director of the Tolstoy Museum and the writer's ex-secretary, commissioned Durylin's memoir about Tolstoy and published it in a collection dedicated on Tolstoy's anniversary. Durylin spent the honorarium on two heavy sheepskin coats that enabled them to leave the house on frosty days.

Durylin managed to publish a few articles in local newspapers and journals, but the honoraria were small and rare. He continued to produce unpublished work: short stories, the chronicle *Kolokola* (The Bells), and to work on the book *In My Own Corner*. In many ways the latter was an "attempt to converse with himself. And about himself. An attempt to understand himself and what happened with him and continued to torture and burn him."[8]

Durylin's letters to his friends were always cheerful. Albeit suffering and ailing, he found the energy to support them morally and discovered ways to help them. In Tomsk he sold Maximilian Voloshin's watercolors (sent to him for that purpose), and transmitted the money back to Koktebel where Voloshin lived without any means (he was able to secure a pension only in 1931—a year before his death).

---

8   G. Pomerantseva, "On Roads and Crossroads," Introduction to Durylin, *In My Own Corner*, 94.

His friends' incessant petitions to mitigate his punishment yielded some results toward the end of 1930: he was able to return from exile and was allowed to settle in one of the seven regional provinces of the USSR. He was not allowed to settle in big cities, however. Durylin chose the town of Kirzhach—closer to Moscow, to native soil. It was much easier to live there than in Tomsk. The conditions were much better, and he also established regular contacts with Moscow. Every week two or three persons would come to visit.

Durylin had a lot of work to do in Kirzhach, and he embarked on it with enthusiasm, but working under a dim kerosene lamp, he completely ruined his vision. For Goethe's centennial he was asked to write a large essay for the *Literaturnoye nalsedstvo* (Literary Legacy) series. Necessary materials were sent to him, including some from Germany in German. In half a year he wrote a lengthy study entitled *Russkie pisateli u Goethe v Weimare* (Russian Writers Visit Goethe in Weimar).[9]

Sergei Nikolaevich's productivity was extraordinary. He could swiftly and simultaneously produce two thematically different kinds of work; his memory was exceptional. But he was incapable of making arrangements for his works to be published. Irina, in addition to doing her usual household chores and receiving guests, began helping Durylin in his work: preparing citations from books, going to Moscow to hand-deliver Durylin's correspondence, taking his papers directly to editorial boards, and bringing back necessary books, as well as Durylin's own manuscripts that had been kept by various acquaintances during his exile. Gradually

---

9   S.N. Durylin, "Russkie pisateli u Goethe v Weimare" (Russian Writers Visit Goethe in Weimar), *Literaturnoye Nasledstvo* 4-6 (1932).

she brought back to the house his whole archive of thirty-five years of scholarly work.

The end of his exile meanwhile was approaching. Before returning to Moscow, Durylin made a formal proposal to marry Irina legally, as it would facilitate their relations with the authorities and people around them. The marriage certificate issued by the town of Kirzhach on July 29, 1933 changed nothing in their relationship, as she remained a spiritual daughter of Rev. Sergei Durylin, but now she was regarded officially as his wife.

At the end of November 1933, Durylin was already in Moscow but Irina was still in Kirzhach, preparing for the move. She packed all their belongings, including books and archival papers, and had them delivered to a railroad storehouse. But it came to pass that the storehouse was burned down on that same December night. Durylin was so shaken by the loss of his personal archives that Irina had to treat him for a nervous disease. She was racking her brains over how to help him out of a deep depression. An accident came to the rescue. At a flea market she bought a used set of the theatrical magazine *Artist* (The Actor) with appendices. She paid all the money she had for it, but was rewarded when she saw how happy Durylin was; he even burst into tears: "I have always dreamed about buying it but never had the money." It was like the finger of God. Durylin's soul began to heal. Irina kept buying him books on theater, as many as she could afford. And he began writing essays for theater journals.

For Durylin this transition to theater studies was natural. He had been an ardent admirer of the Maly and Khudozhestvenny Theaters since his youth. He had collected materials about actors and performances for years. From time to time he had given talks and written articles on theater. He also had written several scripts for dramatizing the works of Russian classic writers.

Durylin's analysis of dramatic works was always linked to their actual stage production. He always organically mixed literary scholarship with theater studies: "Gogol and Theater," "Artyom, Stanislavsky, Chekhov," "History of One Friendship: Ostrovsky and Tchaikovsky," "Gorky on Stage," "Dramaturgy of the Opera in Tsar Nikolai's Epoch," etc. In his book *Pushkin na stsene* (Pushkin in Theater) he for the first time traced the history of Pushkin's drama. Durylin liked to work at the crossroads of the arts, and his broad intellectual scope allowed him to do it. Other published studies included "Repin and Garshin," "Tyutchev in Music," and "Vrubel and Lermontov."

In his biographies of actors Durylin recreated living images on the stage; he did not *describe* an actor's performance but *showed* it. He stressed that a theater scholar should not confuse a literary text that underwent censorship and was aimed at readers with a theatrical one, a prompter's text for the actor to perform. For instance, having found a prompt copy of *Othello* (in which the lead role was played by A.P. Lensky [1847-1908] in the Maly Theater), he observed that the stage direction "he enters [Desdemona's room] with a lantern and warms up his hands" was followed by another note indicating that Lensky emphasized in this scene not Othello's jealousy but his credulousness, which was in line with Pushkin's treatment of this character. Italian actors Salvini or Rossi, when playing Othello, would rush onto the stage at this point, but Lensky just strolled in, experiencing inner torments, and warmed his hands over the lantern. Durylin argued that one cannot adequately review a theater performance by limiting evaluation to just the acting and leaving out any analysis of decorations, costumes, makeup, and music. A reviewer had to be an expert in all these fields, and Durylin certainly was one.

After his return from exile, the efforts by his friends to secure a room for Durylin in Moscow were unsuccessful, but they managed to obtain a lot for building a house in the village of Bolshevo near Moscow. The honorarium he received for the script of Tolstoy's *Anna Karenina* was lavish enough to afford building the house. Durylin wrote it for a Yaroslavl theater but the play was staged in five more cities.

Finally, Durylin was able to acquire his own corner; his hardships, moves, and homelessness were all behind him. Now for the first time in his life he had his own home (he was fifty by then). Irina began by creating a cozy atmosphere in his study: a writing table with a table lamp and inkpot was installed, along with a little leg-rest bench underneath it, ceiling-high bookshelves, a narrow iron bed ("military-style"), and a large sofa. (This atmosphere has been preserved at the Durylin Museum until today.) They also started a little vegetable garden and an orchard. There were two little birch-trees by the study's window. Nadezhda A. Obukhova (1886-1961) sang for Durylin there. He liked to wander about the garden with his guests, recall the Moscow philosophers of the turn of the century, and sit on the bench with M.V. Nesterov, who had his own guest room in the house and would spend several days or even weeks there occasionally.

Everything in the house was arranged to suit Durylin's manner of working. He would get up at dawn, around four in the morning, and sit down in his study to work on his next book, lecture, or presentation. When residents and guests woke up, he would go out to greet them. There was not a single day without someone visiting him.

Sergei Nikolaevich's soul calmed down in Bolshevo under the warm motherly care of Irina. Here he was able to reconcile his clandestine service to God and his open service to art. Durylin's Moscow life was so saturated with literary, scholarly, and pedagogical activities that it appeared as though they were there to compensate for his Tomsk exile. In the mid-1930s he became a senior research associate at the Maly Theater Museum. In 1934, the year when the Soviet Writers' Union was formed, he became a member; his membership ID, number 492, was signed by Maxim Gorky. In 1938 he began collaborating with the Lermontov and Tolstoy groups at the Institute for World Literature (IMLI). At the request of the Institute, Durylin wrote books and articles, gave talks, and participated as a commentator and editor in preparing complete works of classic writers. In 1944 he was awarded a habilitation (PhD) degree at the IMLI without any dissertation defense due to the merit of his publication record.

From May 1945 he was chair of the History of Russian Theater at the State Institute of Theater Art (GITIS); in April 1946 he submitted a request to leave this position and remain a full professor at the department. Numerous dissertations were written and defended under his supervision. In the same period, in March 1945, he became a senior researcher at the Sector of Theater History at the newly introduced Institute for the History of the Arts at the USSR Academy of Sciences. In 1946 he was appointed a lifetime full professor at the Institute. Durylin worked on a number of publications, including writing commentary and entries for the multi-volume *Istoria russkogo teatra* (History of Russian Theater) and for the *Istoria sovetskogo teatra* (History of Soviet Theater).

Up until the end of his life Durylin's prolific work rhythm never slowed down. The Bolshevo period was the most productive one in his career, resulting in more than 200 publications and also a number of works that remained unpublished. He continued writing a series of fundamental studies of the history of literary relations between Russia and Western Europe that began with his work *Russian Writers Visit Goethe in Weimar* and included later essays on "Alexander Dumas, père, and Russia" (1937), "Mme de Staël and her Russian Connections" (1939), etc. In this period he also published large works on the history of literature and theater, as well as several monographs on actors: *Ira Aldridge* (1940), *N.M. Radin* (1941), *P.M. Sadovsky* (1950), and *M.K. Zan'kovetskaya* (1954). For his monograph *M.N. Yermolova* (1953) he was awarded the USSR Academy of Sciences Prize.

A large number of his books and articles were dedicated to the creative legacy of the actors of the Maly and Khudozhestvenny Theaters: M.S. Shchepkin, I.M. Moskvin, V.I. Kachalov, V.N. Pashennaya, O.O. Sadovskaya, P.A. Khokhlov, V.N. Ryzhova, and others. Whoever Durylin wrote about, he never gave up on his principle to first thoroughly study the material, learn everything about the person, the life, the everyday routine, but write only about the creative activity. He wrote exclusively about those who, possessing a talent, were also prominent personalities with a strong moral backbone and a rich spiritual life. He was attracted by bright characters with a rich inner world. Durylin's scholarly gift allowed him to notice many important things that other researchers left unnoticed.

Foreign actors touring in Russia also commanded his attention: Sarah Bernhardt (1844-1923), Eleonora Duse (1858-1924), etc. Durylin became interested in Ira Aldridge, a great actor and skilled performer of the Shakespearean repertoire who had spent a number of years working in Russia, and in doing so, had left a profound influence on Russian actors. He was impressed by Aldridge's combination of fiery temperament, vibrant emotionality, and disciplined self-control. In addition, Aldridge had a sparkling personality.

In 1934 Durylin delivered a lecture at Moscow State University on "Ira Aldridge, a Great Negro Tragedian." It was then that he decided to write a book about the actor. Durylin worked on it for five years, went through six versions, and finally, in 1940, the book came out. His *Ira Aldridge* is still cited by researchers in articles and encyclopedia entries. It is remarkable that as Aldridge was touring Russia, he had performed in some of the same theaters that Durylin visited almost a century later giving lectures and directorial consultations. Durylin also devoted a book, several articles, and lectures to Aldridge's Russian friend, the outstanding actor Mikhail S. Shchepkin (1788-1863). He also wrote on another great actor, Pyotr Sadovsky (1818-1872), who had hospitably welcomed Aldridge at the Maly Theater. Apart from Durylin's book on Aldridge, there are not too many authoritative sources of information on him in Russia, only brief memoirs by sculptor M.O. Mikeshin (1835-1896), lawyer A.F. Koni (1844-1927), and artist Ye.F. Yunge (1843-1913). Recently a few brief Russian-language biographies have appeared on the internet, but their main source of information remains Durylin's book. It should be noted that in many of the Russian cities that Aldridge toured, he is still remembered as a remarkable foreign visitor.

While working on the Aldridge book, Durylin made a truly titanic effort to consult a number of scarce sources, such as newspapers and magazines of the 1850s and 1860s, including those of a number of towns and cities where he performed; he also studied playbills and posters as well as the memoirs of individual spectators that were scattered about various publications or in some cases remained unpublished and kept in archives. As early as in 1907, Durylin's brother Georgii (1888-1949) had recorded recollections of a spectator about Aldridge's performances, and both brothers began collecting newspaper clippings, playbills, and everything else they could locate on the great tragedian. Apparently, Durylin's interest in Aldridge was born back then. The list of cited sources at the end of his book consists of seventy titles. We would argue that in fact it was many more than that.

In the first year of the war — 1941 — the Germans came so close that Durylin subsequently remarked that "the future and present were contained in the now: is this German airplane going to drop a bomb on the roof of our house?" From this "now," Durylin wanted to escape into the remote past, where he longed for "a direct meeting with a long-gone childhood, the stormy days of youth" in the Moscow of the late nineteenth century, and a "lively, light meeting" with father, mother, and nanny. So Durylin began writing his memoirs. His memoir *In My Own Corner* includes his recollections of many of the people who were part of his life: Leo Tolstoy, Rev. Anatoly Optinsky (Potapov), Rev. Alexii Mechev, Vasilii Rozanov (1856-1919), V.A. Kozhevnikov (1852-1917), Rev. Iosif Fudel (1864-1918), among others. These were not just sketches of certain persons but lively narratives about Durylin's relationship with each of them, about events and moments of history, and talks that he recalled. Such autobiographical writing could best be described in Sergei Nikolaevich's own words: "To recollect means to forgive. If one has no power to forgive, one doesn't have to recollect. And this forgiving implies understanding."

He wrote his "reminiscences of the heart," dedicating them to those who should be remembered, not in anguish because they are no longer among the living, but only with gratitude that they did exist.[10]

In 1941-45 a number of Durylin's books were published as part of such series as *Patriotic Writers of the Great Motherland*, *Great Russian People*, and *Library for the Masses*. They included the book *Russian Writers in the Patriotic War of 1812*.[11] Newspapers and magazines published his essays on patriotic subjects: "Heroic Poetry: Mikhail Lermontov," "Gogol and Motherland," "By a Lyre and a Sword," "Idea and Image of Motherland in Russian Literature," etc. Durylin also delivered lectures on patriotism in Russian literature: "Gogol on Popular Heroism," "Pushkin's Patriotism," etc. In addition, he was invited by the Informburo and All-Union Society for Cultural Relations with Abroad (VOKS) to write essays on England and America. In 1946 he was awarded a medal "For Valiant Work during the Patriotic War," and in 1949 he received another decoration—The Order of the Red Banner for Work Efforts.

His Bolshevo period did not yield any documents telling us about the life of his spirit, as was the case before 1930-33. Durylin no longer kept any diaries. His spiritual life remained very intense, but it no longer needed to be described on paper, as he could now recount it in his meetings with his close friends. The friends came to visit often and stayed for several days. They included many actors who came for spiritual support, advice on new roles, as well as information about a particular historical epoch:

---

10 Durylin, *In My Own Corner*, 95.
11 S.N. Durylin, *Russian Writers in the Patriotic War of 1812* (Moscow: Sovetskii Pisatel, 1943).

what people wore, how they walked, how they talked. Sometimes these conversations would turn into rehearsals.

Durylin's house in Bolshevo instantly became a center of gravity for different people but mostly for the Moscow intelligentsia. Around Durylin, intellectual life was always in full swing, involving writers, actors, artists, musicians. Many of them came to quench their spiritual thirst, receive an answer to soul-tormenting questions, find consolation and moral support, or just simply to spend time in an atmosphere of high moral purity and elevated interests, and to rest from the "noble fury" of Soviet reality. Not only did the great erudition of Sergei Nikolaevich attract everyone, but also his kindness, attention and affection for every human being, and his sincerity in communication drew people to him. Durylin liked to socialize with interesting people regardless of their level of education. The main thing was that a person would not be "lazy-minded" nor suffer from a "slavery of thought."

Few of the Moscow intelligentsia of those years failed to attend Durylin's lectures. He always delivered them in a lively manner, taking audiences into the very process of his thoughts, making each of them his personal companion. He regularly made use of new, previously unexplored material. The number of public lectures Durylin delivered in Moscow and other cities on the work of writers and artists was so large that it cannot be determined with certainty. In the House of Scientists, Durylin led a seminar on the history of Russian theater, and in the lecture hall of the Moscow State University, he gave a course of lectures on this subject. He covered a vast range of topics, but, unfortunately, the majority of these lectures and talks have never been published.

Durylin left a very rich archive. He carefully preserved materials on a wide range of his interests, on many creative writers and artists, and gathered a personal library full of important resources, including rare books, autographs, and scarce documents. He also created a huge filing cabinet and a photo library. His portfolio of folders included several hundred items, filled with materials on different topics, notably personalities, theaters, and plays. Here is just one example: from P.P. Pertsov (1868-1947), a major scientist largely neglected by the authorities, Durylin bought Rozanov's letters to him, paying much more for them than was offered by a state institution. He asked Pertsov to write a memoir about Vladimir Solovyov and then bought it from him because Pertsov lived in poverty, without any pension. Durylin came up with a plausible excuse for giving money to Pertsov without offending him: he pretended it was payment for buying some books from him, but in fact he left the books in Pertsov's apartment, having "forgotten" to pick them up.

Providing assistance, supporting people in difficult times—for Durylin and Irina, this was an organic necessity and an integral part of their existence. In the years of famine during the war, they helped many other families with food from their own vegetable garden. They never made a show of all this help. Recently it became known that he had sent money as a monthly pension to M.K. Morozova, a well-known philanthropist before the revolution but then condemned to poverty by the Soviet authorities.

Sergei Durylin died on December 14, 1954. He was sixty-eight years old. Only one and a half years had passed since the death of Stalin, and the Khrushchev thaw was still far away. Durylin could not help but feel the fear of Stalin's repressive "meat grinder" which had destroyed many lives;

this was a kind of suffering to which he was no stranger himself. Preserving and protecting his inner freedom and independence of mind, he wrote a large amount of works "for himself," not hoping to publish them, not even in the future. These works were hidden away deeply in his archives. It was among them that the manuscript of the book *In My Own Corner* was discovered.

Before his death, Durylin told Irina that she could bury him either as a lay person or as a priest—at her own discretion. She buried him as a lay person, because she wanted his writings to be published and his scholarly authority to be preserved. In Kiev, with which Durylin was linked by a number of close friendships and creative threads, his burial service as a priest was conducted in absentia.

It was amazing that hardly had this well-known Russian scholar and popular lecturer died, than his name was banned as if by an invisible hand. Publishers were afraid to publish his work. They took a long time to think it over and decided against it. Irina had the strength of mind, will, and most importantly, faith in God, not to despair, not to lose heart. Now the meaning of her life was in commemorating Durylin's legacy.

In 1959 Irina's efforts helped to open the first and only Bolshevo Public Library. Two thousand volumes from Durylin's personal library were donated to the library. In 1966 it was named after S.N. Durylin. The street leading to the library was also named after him. Memorial tablets have been installed on his house and on the library. In 1993 Irina's sister Aleksandra Vinogradova (1907-1994) opened the S.N. Durylin Memorial House Museum in his Bolshevo house. The museum is now actively functioning, and its staff works on Durylin's large archive and conducts museum tours.

Scholars and researchers turn to his legacy. Magazines and newspapers publish articles about him. Conferences devoted to him are held. His books and articles are published and republished, as are his fictional works. Readers yearning for spiritual and cultural values can now discover this outstanding writer for themselves.

Viktoria N. Toropova

Figure 13: The Durylin Memorial House Museum in winter

Figure 14:the Durylin Memorial House Museum in spring

BIBLIOGRAPHY OF RUSSIAN SOURCES

A., K. "Aldridge on the Russian Stage." *Russkaya Stsena* (The Russian Stage) 8 (1864): 115.

Alekseev, A.A. *Vospominaniya Aktyora A.A. Alekseeva* (Memoirs of Actor A.A. Alekseev). Moscow: Artist, 1894.

Almazov, B. "Aldridge on the Moscow Stage." *Russkii Vestnik* (Russian Bulletin) 40 (1862): 12-13.

_____. "Aldridge on the Moscow Stage." *Russkii Vestnik* (Russian Bulletin) 41 (1862): 11-13.

Almedingen, N. "Po povodu ozhidaemogo priezda v Saratov Oldridzha (Regarding Aldridge's Upcoming Arrival in Saratov)." *Spravochny Listok* (Saratov Newsletter) 141 (1854).

Anon. "Phelka (Little Bee)." *Severnaya Pchela* (Northern Bee) 254 (November 17, 1858): 1070.

Anon. "Phelka (Little Bee)." *Severnaya Pchela* (Northern Bee) 259 (November 24, 1858): 1089.

Anon. "[Caricatures]." *Syn Otechestva* (Son of the Fatherland) 49 (December 7, 1858): 1487.

Anon. "A Page from the Diary of an Old Theatergoer." *Severnaya Pchela* (Northern Bee) 278 (December 17, 1858): 1165.

Anon. "Aldridge in *Othello*." *Nashe Vremya* (Our Time) 203 (September 21, 1862): 811.

Anon. "Ira Aldridge as Shylock." *Nashe Vremya* (Our Time) 210 (September 30, 1862): 839.

Anon. "[First Performance of *Othello*]." *Saratovskie Gubernskie Vedomosti* (Saratov Provincial Gazette) 31 (July 11, 1864): 306.

Anon. "Aldridge in Tambov: Local News." *Tambovskie Gubernskie Vedomosti* (Tambov Provincial Gazette) 43 (October 1864): 341.

Anon. "Kazan." *Russkaya Stsena* (The Russian Stage) 4/5 (1865): 247-48.

Anon. "[Ticket Prices]." *Odesskie Novosti* (Odessa News) 12 (January 18, 1866).

Anon. "Aldridge as Othello." *Odesskie Novosti* (Odessa News) 20 (January 27, 1866).

Anon. "[Note]." *Antrakt* (Intermission) 34 (September 4, 1866).

Anon. "Biographical Anecdotes: Aldridge and Smirnov." *Souffleur* 75 (October 2, 1880).

Anon. "Correspondence of Aksakov with N.S. Sokhanskaya (Kokhanovskaya)." *Russkoe obozrenie* (Russian Review) 45 (1897): 530-31.

Anon. "[Correspondence from Washington]." *Izvestia VTSIK* 152 (June 30, 1935).

Arapov, Pimen Nikolaevich. *Letopis Russkago Teatra* (Chronicle of the Russian Theater). St. Petersburg: Tip N. Tiblena i komp, 1861.

Bakhrushin, A.A., and N.L. Brodsky, eds. *Neizdannye pis'ma k A.N. Ostrovskomu* (Unpublished Letters to A.N. Ostrovsky). Moscow: Academia, 1932.

Balakirev, M.A. *Perepiska M.A. Balakireva s V.V. Stasovym* (Correspondence of M.A. Balakirev with Stassov). Petrograd: T/D. Lemberg, 1917.

Barsukov, Nikolay Platonovich. *Zhizn' i trudy M.P. Pogodina* (Pogodin's Life and Works. St. Petersburg: M.M. Stasiulevich, 1902.

———. "Nizhny Novgorod Notes." *Teatr* 5 (1939): 134-37.

Batalin, I.L. "Theater of Kaluga." *Russkaya Stsena (The Russian Stage)* 12 (1864): 187.

Bazhenov, Aleksandr Nikolaevich. *Sochinenia i Perevod* (Collected Works and Translations). Moscow: Tip Kosogorova, 1869. Vol. 1.

Berdyaev, N.A. *Samopoznanie* (Self-Cognition). Moscow: Eksmo 2006.

Bertenson, Sergei L'vovich. *Ded russkoi stseny* (Grandfather of the Russian Stage). Petrogad: Mitjurnikov in Komm., 1916.

Chernyshevsky, Nikolay Gavrilovich. *Polnoe sobranie sochineniy* (Complete Works). St. Petersburg: M.N. Chernyshevskago, 1906. Vol. 8 and 9.

Dalmatov, V.P. "Aldridge na yarmarke: rasskaz iz zapisnoi knizhki (Aldridge at the Fair. A Story from my Notebook)." *Niva* 20 (1896): 736.

Davydov, V.N. *Rasskaz o proshlom* (A Story about the Past). Moscow-Leningrad: Academia, 1930.

De-Ribas, Alexandr. *Staraya Odessa* (The Old Odessa). Odessa: Kraft, 1913.

Dobrotvor, N.M. *Taras Shevchenko v N. Novgorode: Spornik* (Taras Shevchenko in Nizhny Novgorod: A Collection). [Gorky]: Gorky Regional Press, 1939.

Durylin, S.N. "Russkie pisateli u Goethe v Weimare." (Russian Writers Visit Goethe in Weimar). *Literaturnoye Nasledstvo* 4-6 (1932).

_____. *Russian Writers in the Patriotic War of 1812*. Moscow: Sovetskii Pisatel, 1943.

_____. *Rus prikrovennaya* (The Secret Rus). Moscow: Palomnik, 2000.

_____. *In My Own Corner*. Moscow: Molodaya Gvardia, 2006. This 879-page book was initially published in 1991 in an abbreviated form.

_____. "From the Olonets Notes." *Nashe Nasledie* (Our Legacy) 100 (2011): 133-55.

Florensky, P.A. "Correspondence with M.A. Novosyolov." In *Rev. Pavel Florensky's Archives*. Tomsk: Vodolei, 1998. 2:24.

Gatsisky, A.S. *Nizhegorodski Teatr 1798-1867* (Nizhny Novgorod Theater 1798-1867). Nizhny Novgorod: Tipografia gubernskogo pravlenia,1867.

Gertso-Vinogradskii, S.T. "Mr. Ira Aldridge in the role 'Richard III.'" *Odesskii Vestnik* (Odessa Bulletin) 30 (1866): 95-96.

G-fov, A. "Theater Chronicle." *Teatralny i Muzikalny Vestnik* (Theatrical and Musical Bulletin) 49 (December 13, 1859): 483.

Goltz-Miller, I. "The Black Tragedian and the White Audience." *Odesskie Novosti* (Odessa News) 21 (February 3, 1866).

Grigoriev, Apollon. *Vospominaniya* (Memoirs). Moscow and Leningrad: Academia, 1930.

Herzen, Alexandr Ivanovic. *Byloe i Dumy* (My Past and Thoughts). Moscow: Academia, 1932. Vol. 3.

I., A. "In Saratov." *Volga* 40 (September 5, 1864): 149.

Karneev, M. "Dva slova po povodu *Othello* (A Few Words Regarding *Othello* on the Stage of the Maly Theater)." *Yezhegodnik imperatorskikh teatrov* (Yearbook of the Imperial Theaters) (1907-08).

Katin. "Notes on Moscow Life." *Razvlechenie* (Entertainment) 39 (September 20, 1862): 156-57.

Kokhanskaya, N.S. "Aldridge-Othello" [letter to the editor]. *Den'* (Day) 39 (September 29, 1862): 17-18.

Koni, A.F. "Iz dalyokogo proshlogo" (From the Remote Past). In *Sto let Malomu teatru 1824-1924* (Maly Theater Centennial), ed. Alexandr Rafailovich Kugel. Moscow: Russkoe Teatralnoe Obshchestvo, 1924.

Kublitsky, M.E. "P.S. Mochalov." *Russkii Arkhiv* (Russian Archive) 12 (1875): 487.

Lensky, A.P. "Notes of an Actor." *Artist* 36 (1894): 100.

Leontovsky, V.M. "At M.S. Shchepkin's." *Moskovskie Vedomosti* (Moscow Gazette) 116 (1895).

M., V. "Feuilleton." *Spravochnyi listok g[ubernii] Saratova* (Directory of the [Province] of Saratov) 128 (June 18, 1864): 2.

Monumentov, Vladimir. "Aldridge in Moscow. A Lyrical Scene." *Razvlechenie* (Entertainment) 41 (October 11, 1862): 190.

Nadimov-Shamshenko, P.M. "Vospominaniya Aktyora" (Memoirs of an Actor). Manuscript No. 1016. A.A. Bakhrushin Theater Museum, Moscow.

Nazarov, N.S. "Aldridge in *King Lear*." *Russkii Vestnik* (Russian Bulletin) 42 (1862): 25.

Nesterov, M.V. *Letters*. Leningrad: Iskusstvo, 1988.

Panaev, I.I. "Petersburg Life: Notes of a New Poet." *Sovremennik* (Contemporary) 72, Nos. 11-12 (1858): 260.

Panovsky, N. "What is Going on in Moscow." *Russkii Vestnik* (Russian Bulletin) 38 (September 1862): 30-31.

Pasternak, B.L. *Izbrannoye* (Selected Works). Moscow: Chudozestvannaya Literatura, 1985). Vol. 2.

Pisemsky, A.F. *Pisma* (Letters). Moscow: Academy of Sciences, 1936.

Polevoi, K.A. "Theatrical Chronicle: Mr. Samoilov and Mr. Ira Aldridge in the Role of Shakespeare's Lear." *Severnaya Pchela* (Northern Bee) 287 (December 31, 1858): 1201-2.

Pomerantseva, G. "On Roads and Crossroads." Introduction to Durylin, *In My Own Corner*.

Rodislavsky, V.I. "Aldridge and His Performances in Kazan." *Russkaya Stsena* (The Russian Stage) 4/5 (1865): 97-113.

Schuking, L. "Negro Actor." *Pantheon* 10, No. 5 (1858): 77.

Sinelnikov, Nikolai Nikolaevich. *Shestdesyat let na Stsene. Zapiski* (Sixty Years on Stage. Notes). [Kharkov]: Idatelstvo Kharkovskogo gos. teatra russkoi dramy, 1936.

Sokolov, D.I. "Penza Theater." *Penzenskie Gubernskie Vedomosti* (Penza Provincial Gazette) 50 (1864): 331-33.

Stakhovich, A.A. *Klochki vospominaniy* (Scraps of Memories). Moscow: N. Kushnerev, 1904.

Strepetova, P.A. *Vospominaniya i pisma* (Memoirs and Letters). Moscow: Academia, 1934.

Urusov, A.I. *Statyi, pisma, vospominaniya* (Articles, Letters, Reminiscences). Moscow: I.N. Kohlchev, 1907. Vol. 1.

Velizarii, M.I. *Put Provintsialnoi aktrisy* (A Provincial Actress's Path). Leningrad and Moscow: Iskusstvo, 1938.

Verbitskaya, Anastasia Alekseevna. *Moemy chitateliu* (To My Reader). Moscow: I.N. Kushnerev, 1908.

Yanzhul, I.I. *Memories of Things Seen and Experienced in 1864-1909*. St. Petersburg: Electro-tipografiya N.I. Stoikovoi, 1910.

Yunge, Ye.F. *Vospominaniya 1843-1860* (Memoirs of Ye.F. Yunge, née Countess Tolstaya, 1843-1863). St. Petersburg: Sphinx, 1913.

Zakharyin, I.N. *Meetings and Memoirs*. St. Petersburg: M.V. Pirozkova, 1903.

Zaslavsky, D.O. *Essays on the History of North American United States, 18th and 19th Centuries*. Moscow: Ogonek, 1931.

Zotov. R. "Petersburg Chronicle: The African Tragedian Aldridge in Shakespeare's *Othello*." *Sankpeterburgskie Vedomosti* (St. Petersburg Official Gazette) 252 (November 16, 1858): 1478.

_____. "Social Notes." *Syn Otechestva* (Son of the Fatherland) 48 (November 30, 1858): 53.

_____. " Social Notes." *Syn Otechestva* (Son of the Fatherland) 1 (January 4, 1859): 4.

Zvantsov, K.I. *Ira Aldridge: Essay on His Life and Performances*. St. Petersburg: Ya. Ionson, 1858.

_____. "Aldridge's Debut in Othello." *Teatralny i Muzikalny Vestnik* (Theatrical and Musical Bulletin) 45 (November 16, 1858): 530-31.

_____. "2. The Merchant of Venice." *Teatralny i Muzikalny Vestnik* (Theatrical and Musical Bulletin) 46 (November 23, 1858.): 545-46.

_____. "*King Lear*." *Teatralny i Muzikalny Vestnik* (Theatrical and Musical Bulletin) 48 (December 7, 1858): 565.

_____. "Mr. Ira Aldridge's Benefit." *Teatralny i Muzikalny Vestnik* (Theatrical and Musical Bulletin) 51 (December 28, 1858): 602.

INDEX

==============☙==============

311014-200-2-60W